FIFTEEN YOUNG MEN

FIFTEEN YOUNG MEN

AUSTRALIA'S UNTOLD FOOTBALL TRAGEDY

PAUL KENNEDY

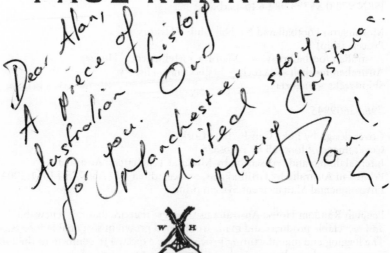

Dear Alan,
A piece of history for you. Our Australian Manchester United story.
Merry Christmas.
Paul.

WILLIAM HEINEMANN: AUSTRALIA

A William Heinemann book
Published by Penguin Random House Australia Pty Ltd
Level 3, 100 Pacific Highway, North Sydney NSW 2060
www.penguin.com.au

Penguin
Random House
Australia

First published by William Heinemann in 2016

Addresses for the Penguin Random House group of companies can be found at global.penguinrandomhouse.com/offices.

National Library of Australia
Cataloguing-in-Publication entry

Kennedy, Paul, author
Fifteen young men/Paul Kennedy

ISBN 978 0 85798 982 6 (paperback)

Mornington Football and Netball Club – History
Process (ship)
Australian football players – Victoria – Melbourne – History
Australian football – Victoria – Melbourne – History
Shipwrecks – Victoria

796.33609945

Cover design by Luke Causby/Blue Cork
Cover image of football by Fotosearch
Internal design and typesetting by Midland Typesetters, Australia
Printed in Australia by Griffin Press, an accredited ISO AS/NZS 14001:2004 Environmental Management System printer

Penguin Random House Australia uses papers that are natural, renewable and recyclable products and made from wood grown in sustainable forests. The logging and manufacturing processes are expected to conform to the environmental regulations of the country of origin.

In memory of a lost teammate:
Donny Epa, 1985–2010;
and for *my* three sons

‘Life is an obligation which friends often owe to each other
in the wilderness.’
– James Fenimore Cooper, *Last of the Mohicans*

Preface

There. Something on the reef, near the point.

The searchers – half-a-dozen local fishermen in three small boats – looked northward to a dark object floating in the silver bay. They sailed closer to their discovery in dismal silence.

It was the *Process* but not as they remembered her. The small yacht had been beaten and busted, as if by a cyclone; both masts were splintered, ropes and mainsail entangled a few inches below the surface, and the timber hull was vertical, wobbling in the current like a half-empty bottle of whiskey. The bow was four feet high because of the air trapped under the forward half-deck.

Dressed in heavy coats and low hats, the fishermen dropped their canvases when they were close enough to inspect the damage, careful not to go too close. They did not want to be cursed.

Now they saw discarded clothing – jackets, trousers, vests,

red-and-white football jerseys – mixed up in the flotsam and jetsam. But where were the captain Charles Hooper and the rest of the football team: those fifteen young men?

Such a wretched scene many miles from land would give no hope of finding survivors. But the *Process* was just a few hundred yards from dry rocks and sand. Most of the team could swim; many of the younger players had grown up duck-diving off piers and jetties and at the local baths. Hooper, who had spent his lifetime fishing and sailing Port Phillip, was so strong in the water he was said to be 'good for five miles or more'.

Well, if any of them had made it to the beach they were not standing there, waving back at the fishermen. The usually handsome cliff coastline looked bare and mean.

Among the speechless search party was Charles Hooper's brother and fishing partner, Fred, at the helm of the *Progress* (the sister craft of the one floating in miserable fragments), wondering how he would explain to the rest of his family what he was seeing. Dread was also choking the other witnesses; they knew the missing as if they were kin. Most had grown up together – sons of pioneers – in the streets, churches, creek beds, orchards, stables, paddocks and picnic parks of their nearby hometown, once called Schnapper Point – now Mornington.

'They've found something!' echoed a distant voice.

Fred Hooper and the others turned to see who had shouted and saw the famous yacht *Wanderer*, her many sails stretched wide, approaching as fast as the breeze allowed.

The *Wanderer* had been anchored in Mornington harbour for Queen's Birthday weekend; her owner, businessman-adventurer Henry Fergie, was on his last cruise of the season, hosting some Melbourne gentlemen for a few days of smoke, wine, oysters, teal, pickled pork and plum pudding. Fergie had quit breakfast and acted quickly on a request to help find the *Process* and her crew of beloved footballers.

Upon the *Wanderer*'s crosstrees stood the great sailor Arthur Peck, looking through his marine glasses.

'They've found something,' Peck bellowed again. 'Make fast for it.'

The fishermen were relieved by the prospect of help from experienced hands. Fergie and Peck had conquered oceans and would not be as easily spooked by the wreckage. They'd know what to do. On arriving, Peck helped fasten two of the fishing boats to the *Wanderer*'s stern and asked Fred Hooper for a small anchor to be used as a grapnel. His aim was to make the *Process* horizontal again so it could be towed to Mornington.

Several times he threw the steel hook, trying to latch onto the bow. Finally, it held. Peck yanked tight the line. Others hurried to help. The water was heavy and it took a long time but eventually they lifted the *Process*, at least enough to expose part of the hull. Then they saw the scratch marks.

The boat's white paint and golden racing stripe had been shredded to the wood, as if gnawed by sharks.

Peck, Fergie, Fred Hooper and all the other fishermen knew immediately that the tearing was not from teeth but fingernails, symbols of a desperate human struggle. The awful sight made sense of the other carnage; the mizzenmast had been broken off and the centreboard had suffered under enormous weight. It was obvious the team had spent minutes, maybe hours, clutching and clawing the craft with cold, stiffening fingers.

Elevating the boat slightly was possible but bringing her to an even keel was not. It felt like something was holding her down. After an hour of effort, the retrievers were all out of breath, defeated. The wind started to chop up the bay and the *Process* bumped the *Wanderer*, whose crew used poles to separate the two. Someone suggested there might be ballast in the wrecked boat's stern. There was. One of the fishermen banished dark thoughts, climbed in and found loose bars of metal. He threw them overboard. Peck and the others took the line attached to the grapnel and heaved and the *Process* came up and over. Air rushed from her bow and the boat was righted, though still submerged.

Then they saw him.

A naked body was lying, one knee raised, bent over the gunwale.

Two more fishermen swallowed hard on their fears and stepped down into the craft to free the corpse. They saw a rope that was tied so firmly around the dead man's thigh it had sliced into his skin. Peck passed a knife. One of the fishermen reached in to make the cut. At the same time a small wave rushed through and turned the body to reveal a familiar face.

'It's Alfred Lawrence,' someone said. 'He's the storekeeper's son.'

Alfred's brown eyes were open. His expression was peaceful.

The fishermen backed off and refused to touch the body

again. Gentlemen from the *Wanderer* had to climb in and take Alfred Lawrence out of the *Process*; they lifted him into one of the other boats. After the scattered clothing was fished from the sea, the fleet began its journey home. The *Wanderer* – flag lowered – towed the waterlogged wreck behind its dinghy, careful not to go too fast 'for fear of carrying away the bow of the Process'.

Henry Fergie would later recall in his logbook: 'We arrived some time in front of the other boats and found a crowd of anxious friends of the missing men congregated on the end of jetty eager to learn the worst.'

By now, everyone in town was aware the football team had not come home. Hundreds remained at the harbour for a search update but not all could endure the torture of waiting. Some men had headed north along the high coastline hoping to find survivors. Dozens of women, wearing dresses too cumbersome to lift through the twisted ti-tree foreshore, stayed nearer the shopfronts or along the Esplanade, press-lipped, nodding and shaking their heads at each other, some trembling in the premature winter. Others had heard the bells and gone to church, though no one knew if the minister would come. It had become well known that three of Reverend James Caldwell's sons – Jim, Willie and Hugh – were lost with the rest of the team. But the old Irishman with the long, white beard had not missed a sermon, or any important social event, in almost twenty years.

Reverend Caldwell, one of the most revered citizens of Mornington since his arrival in 1874, turned every head in Main Street as he walked in his dark three-piece suit and overcoat from the foreshore up the slight rise of the thoroughfare, past the hotels, boarding houses, police station, white-picketed Mechanics' Institute, butcher, baker, smithy's, general stores, toward the St Andrew's Presbyterian chapel.

He paused near the football field, where one of his sons had only recently commanded centre stage during an exciting match – perhaps the most thrilling contest the peninsula ever hosted. All in the district remembered that sodden day.

Saturday afternoons had been given to local football since 1887. At first, the games were a jaunt. But within a few seasons, the men's ego and pride had made contests serious fun. By 1891 footballers of 'The Point' (as locals liked to call Mornington) had been dragged into a community-wide class dispute. Socially, the 'workers' wanted nothing more to do with the 'toffs' so they had formed their own committee and team: Rovers. Most Australian towns didn't have a football club at the start of the 1890s; because of its bickering, Mornington had two.

The first intra-village grudge match between 'Mornington' and 'Rovers' gave spectators anxiety and goosebumps. Against predictions, the game was close and, in fact, the new mob led by a goal with minutes, if not seconds, to go.

Barrackers crowded the boundary in a state of near-apoplexy, pushing and spilling onto the field, which was a grubbed farm. Women in woollen dresses, tweed overcoats, stitched brim hats, and carrying team-coloured parasols hollered for their favoured side to kick another goal. Children, previously distracted by jumping in puddles, began screaming. An invasion of the oval, not at all unusual in Australian rules football, seemed likely.

'Keep back,' called the umpire, affable local police officer Senior Constable Thomas Murphy.

Penned in by the ruckus, the players were so tired by now they could barely run. The game's bounce and flow had gone. It had become a routine of two groups of men in knickerbockers and thick-heeled boots, ponging of dirt, sweat, spit and blood, chasing the ball or whoever held it. Jerseys had been fouled by mud so it was hard to identify players. Out of context, the game at this point might have seemed pointless, if not stupid. No one could hold the ball long enough to use it cleverly. Anyone who picked it up was scratched, tackled and belted until he lost it or gave it away. Not that there was any real violence left in the game. By this fourth quarter, even the collisions had become second-rate.

Members of the Rovers club had surprised even themselves by taking the lead earlier in the half. Victory and all it would bring now looked probable.

The timekeeper reached for the cowbell.

There was a chance for *maybe* one last surge at the goals. A Mornington player picked up the leather ball and ran with it; the congestion in front of the Rovers' goalposts meant scoring was only possible if someone could take a mark and was allowed time and space to shoot over the defenders' heads.

About to be snared, the player carrying the ball punted it into the air. The oval projectile was damp and hard and didn't travel far before falling like a shot quail. A hundred yards away, the crowd inhaled.

If no one took a mark the Rovers would win the game. But someone did.

It was Rev. Caldwell's teenage son Hugh.

'Hughie's got it!'

The cowbell rang: DING. DING. DING. DING. DING.

Hats of all shapes and heights were thrown into the air. Roaming play was finished but the match would not be completed until after Hugh Caldwell's kick. He could not win it for his team but a greater motivator than victory has always been to avoid defeat. A draw was still possible.

At sixteen, Hugh was one of the finest teenage athletes in the colony. Broad-shouldered with long arms, he had the body of a twenty-one-year-old. His round, soft-eyed face was still boyish. His skin glowed olive and his flat hair was parted without flourish.

The Rovers' barrackers shook their heads.

'He can't kick it from there,' one said.

'No one could at such a distance.'

But he could. He was of the first generation of boys who had grown up with the game of Australian rules. A ball rested in his hands as easily as a horseman in his saddle.

Everyone, including friends and family, ran over to Hugh, who was calm and half-smiling. He noticed his older brother Tom and sister Alice standing nearby. Another brother, Willie, was on his team. So was his best friend, Charlie Allchin, youngest son of one of the town's founding English parents. Hugh and Charlie had spent more time together in childhood than most siblings – the Australian version of Huck Finn and Tom Sawyer.

They shared a cheeky glance.

Teammates huddled around the drama's lead actor. There was baker Tom Coxhell, bank manager Henry Short, fisherman Charles Hooper, carpenter William Grover, storekeeper's son Alfred Lawrence, blacksmith Willie Coles, telegraph operator John Kinna . . .

Senior Constable Murphy blew his whistle, grabbed Hugh by the shoulders and escorted him to his starting position, wished him luck.

Almost everyone had witnessed that next kick from the minister's happiest son. Only Rev. Caldwell missed the game's climax. The man whose children called him 'Papa' was at home writing the next day's sermon; he had never cared for sport, yet he always liked to hear of his son's feats.

His dear sons.

Three of them were gone, never to come home. Or might they? If anyone could make it back to land from a boating accident it would be Hughie, he thought. Willie, too, had a chance, but maybe not poor Jim, who would have been so tired from his cross-country trek the week leading up to the game.

The minister arrived at his orange-brick church under the eucalyptus trees and entered as he had done every Sunday for eighteen years. The pews were crowded with families he knew better than anyone. He looked down at them looking up at him – most seated but some standing at the rear – and could see faces begging answers. *Is it really true? What do we do now? How could this happen? What chances do the rest of them have?*

Reverend Caldwell knew the burden of private grief. His first two wives, his first baby . . . but this was different. He removed his jacket, his hat. He arranged his notes and cleared his throat, opened his mouth, but could find no words. The townspeople's questions were also his. And he had one more: *Oh, why did we come to this fatal paradise in the first place?*

1

Finding Schnapper Point

One

Like Rev. Caldwell, the first Europeans to arrive at Port Phillip adored its splendour but were cautious of its dangers and moods, so white settlement came slowly. Also, it took a while for them to find the place.

The British Empire started mapping the southern coast of Australia in the late eighteenth century. By then, the penal settlement of Sydney (Port Jackson) was brimful of convicts; colonial chiefs were starting to worry about the population's morale and morality. A second settlement was needed.

Among the best explorers at that time was a handsome surgeon called George Bass, who took six volunteers in a banksia-timber boat to explore the theory among seamen that a treacherous passage of water separated the Australian mainland and Tasmania (Van Diemen's Land). He proved it right.

Bass Strait was immediately recognised as a fearful section of the coast but rich with resources, waiting to be exploited;

sealers and whalers came in a hurry and started living on small islands and headlands. Sydney sent experienced ship commanders, including Scot Lieutenant James Grant, to scout possible settlement locations. Grant and his party came to a significant bay (Western Port) but knew it could not support a new colony.

It was Grant's replacement aboard the famous *Lady Nelson*, Lieutenant John Murray, who later sailed further west and found a gap in the land that hinted at a much larger port.

Murray was hesitant to sail through the break in the coast – later known as The Heads – because of its sharp rocks and swirling tides. He waited outside for a calmer swell, mapping King Island in his spare time. But he had to move soon; the pressure on the officer to find a settlement was increasing. Two French ships, *Naturaliste* and *Geographe*, had been seen in southern Australian waters, unnerving Murray's masters in London. Eventually, he chose not to risk destroying the *Lady Nelson*. In January 1802, he sent his first mate, William Bowen, upon a launch with five armed men and provisions. With rare skill, Bowen sailed through The Heads and was floored by what appeared to be an inland sea. This 'noble sheet of water', as Bowen later described it, would be named Port Phillip after Australia's first governor.

The bay of Port Phillip is a natural freak in the shape of a giant frying pan. Its size – coastline 260 kilometres – and modest depth – up to 24 metres – make it unique to any country. The rest of the southern hemisphere has nothing that compares. On first impression, it seemed a settlement certainty. Bowen went to the eastern shores and found white beaches and salt-trimmed bluffs and was taken by their beauty. When conditions were right, he sailed back into Bass Strait to report to Murray, who made tentative plans to sail the *Lady Nelson* through the foreboding channel for a first-hand inspection.

He was right to remain nervous. About four per cent of Port Phillip's water spills into the ocean every tide, meaning the bay is still emptying even as the tide is coming in. The water moving through at a top speed of eight knots creates an orgy of rips and whirlpools. Only when the bay and Bass Strait are at equal heights is the entrance calm. But that lasts about the time it takes to drink a cup of tea. Then the surge starts again. Murray waited another ten days. Then, blood up, the lieutenant navigated his way into the expanse of water that would one day transform the world's economy.

Murray anchored in the shallows and rowed to land. He climbed a mountain lookout, naming it Arthur's Seat, and surveyed the land between Port Phillip and Western Port, a peninsula of hills and valleys that 'rise and fall with inexpressible elegance . . .'

During his twenty-five-day stay, Murray made contact – and danced – with the local Indigenous people: Boon Wurrung (also spelled Bunurung or Boonoorung), one of five Kulin nation tribes. He wanted to learn where he could find fresh water. The Boon Wurrung men were interested in the white men's guns and did not believe it when told 'they were only walking sticks'.

One meeting of 'friendly intercourse' turned deadly when

tribesmen with spears ambushed Murray's crew on a beach. Bowen shot his gun as a warning. Murray later wrote in his log, 'This was found only to create a small Panic and our party were oblidg'd to teach them by fatal experience the effect of our Walking Sticks.' Three Boon Wurrung men were shot.

The ambush convinced Murray the Boon Wurrung was a savage tribe but it was not. The attack was most likely revenge for the crimes committed on the locals by some of the white-skinned sealers, or 'cut-throats' as historians have called them. In truth, the Boon Wurrung was a mostly peaceable, semi-nomadic tribe.

Before returning to Sydney to file a report on what he had seen, Murray held a flag-raising ceremony, a declaration this port and peninsula now belonged to His Sacred Majesty, King George III.

The next commander to arrive at Port Phillip was the outstanding Matthew Flinders. He came three months after Murray and sailed the *Investigator* through The Heads, passing its test. Flinders followed Murray's route up the eastern beaches, giving a five-star review of the land.

Then the explorer went further north. A few miles away he found an exquisite stretch of rock inlets overseen by rich ochre cliffs. One small harbour was the prettiest, spectacular from a dozen different angles. He stopped nearby and scaled a bluff that protected a horseshoe beach. It was midday, 29 April 1802, temperature cool. The bay shone in the autumn light.

Flinders had found the spot for a town that would one day be called Mornington, where you can look across Port Phillip every twilight at the sun sinking beneath rainbow clouds and imagine you are staring at a blue expanse no less impressive than the majestic Indian Ocean.

After Flinders' visit and subsequent recommendation it was clear to colonial chiefs they had located the best port for a new colony. But where should they set up camp?

In the summer of 1803, Sydney-based Governor Philip King sent to Port Phillip a surveying party, which found a broad waterway at the bay's northern tip. They called it both the 'Great River' and the 'Freshwater River' (later the Yarra River), home to swans, pelicans and ducks. But the 'most eligible place for a settlement' was not to be used for another thirty-three years. The British Government had already moved to create a penal settlement near The Heads. Colonel David Collins, a sociable but strict officer with the Royal Marines, was given the task of relocating convicts, free settlers and soldiers to Port Phillip; he selected property near the place Murray had raised his flag and called it Sullivan Bay.

The settlement of 307 convicts arrived on two ships and lasted only months. Clearing the land was easy enough but cultivating wheat was tricky. Digging for water was also difficult. Chagrin led to prison breaks.

Most absconders were captured by soldiers and punished. But one runaway remained free: William Buckley. Buckley thrived in the bush by living with the Wada wurrung (or Wathaurung) tribe, friends of the Boon Wurrung.

There were some moments of joy in the first Port Phillip settlement. A baby was born. A free woman married a convict. Collins' officers fished for stingrays, hunted kangaroos, and smoked their pipes watching summer storms come at them from Bass Strait.

But Collins was convinced the colony would never succeed. He wrote to Governor King, 'The sooner we are enabled to leave this unpromising and unproductive country, the sooner we shall be able to reap the advantages of a more fertile spot.' On 23 January 1804, he ordered all his charges back onto the ships and took them to Van Diemen's Land, where he founded and ruled Hobart Town.

It was another thirty-one years before Europeans returned to Port Phillip with intentions to settle. In 1835, a band of rich pastoralists, led by ambitious John Batman, created the 'Port Phillip Association', which aimed to compel the Kulin nation elders to sign an illegal treaty for settlement of land surrounding Port Phillip. Batman wanted to live along the banks of the same 'Freshwater River' the surveying party had recommended decades earlier. Of the Yarra, Batman wrote, 'I am glad to state, about six miles up found the river all good water and very deep. This will be the place for a village.'

One of the first people to greet Batman in Port Phillip was the runaway William Buckley, wearing a kangaroo-skin rug. Buckley was recruited as a go-between, helping Batman with his deal: the transfer of hundreds of thousands of acres for 'one hundred pair of blankets one hundred knives one hundred tomahawks fifty suits of clothing fifty looking glasses fifty pair scissors and five tons flour.'

So Melbourne was born.

For the next two decades settlers came to Port Phillip and spread out like sheep in a paddock. Some chose to stay in the new city; others rode into the country to farm. When gold fever overcame the population and drew fortune hunters from around the world, diggers started living in the burgeoning towns of Ballarat, Beechworth and Bendigo, or in tiny tent villages with strange names like 'Slaughter Yard Hill' or 'New Chum Gully'.

There was no gold in the southern peninsula that Matthew Flinders had found so admirable. That coastline remained relatively unpopulated by Europeans until the middle of the 1850s.

The mothers and fathers of The Point arrived soon after.

Two

Englishwoman Sarah Jagger was in her late twenties when she saw the sway and promise of the ocean. It was 1855 and she had come immaculately dressed to Bristol in search of a ship. She wanted to go to Australia.

Once home to the world's biggest merchant vessels, Bristol was now a medium-sized port wearing rough from overuse. Sarah perused many tied-up ships, from the elegant to the undignified. She enquired about passage. The smiling captain of one of the shoddiest boats in the harbour came to her and offered a berth, claiming he had room for one more. She took only a glance at his horrid craft.

'No, thank you,' she said.

Next to tap Sarah's shoulder was a friendly clergyman. He knew of a ship and would arrange her safe travel if she agreed to his terms.

'I have a family of eight young people going out to meet

their father in Melbourne,' said the minister. 'Their only protector is a grandma of eighty.'

Sarah nodded. She had made her living caring for the young and old; it would not be easy work, and she hinted to the clergyman she would need convincing. 'Oh, do go with them,' he said. 'God will bless you for it. And their father will be sure to reward you.'

Sarah went to see the ship being proposed: *Rajah of Sarawak*. Tall and impressive, it could not have been in better condition. She said yes, paid forty-six pounds for a first-class ticket, prepared her luggage and waited to sail. A high tide was needed for departure. On Thursday 5 July, the water rose mid-morning and the *Rajah* released from its anchorage. With the ebbing swell, she went toward the Celtic Sea. So began a five-month journey to Sarah's mysterious new home.

Many had died trying to make it to Australia in those hurried years after gold was found in the colonies. Ships from England were often overcrowded and disease ridden. Children were most vulnerable. Eighty-three of them died aboard a vessel called the *Bourneuf* in 1852. The *Marco Polo* lost forty-six under the age of four. Then came a greater tragedy. Made in New York, the *Ticonderoga* was hired by the United Kingdom's 'Emigration Commission' to transport people and provisions to Melbourne. In 1852 it carried almost 800 passengers – mostly Scottish highlanders – from Liverpool to Port Phillip. More than a hundred people died before the ship – 'carrying the stench of death' – reached The Heads. Immigration officers found maggots had overrun the lower sleeping quarters. Surviving passengers later explained they had witnessed crew wrap bodies in bedding and throw them overboard.

Sarah was wise enough to have chosen a clean sailing ship that differed to the *Ticonderoga* in every way. Though heavy fogs and waves made her 'senses rock' for the first three days, she recovered quickly. The captain, Sheppard Giles Esq. Commander, gave comfort by reading prayers aloud every night.

Come unto me all ye that are weary and heavy laden and I will give you rest.

As the *Rajah* made its way to the South Atlantic Ocean, Sarah taught the children in her care how to make hand towels from tablecloths. Needlework was her expertise. The previous year she had planned to open a children's dress shop in London before a family crisis had compelled her to the sea.

A lady of soft, refined features, Sarah Jagger was born in London. She had five siblings from her father's two marriages. Her dad, Jabez, was a trained solicitor but never practised law. One day, a gun exploded in his hand. After recovering from his injuries, he opened and managed a successful drapery. After his first wife died, he met and married a woman called Elizabeth Wilson – Sarah's mother.

Fire later destroyed the drapery. The shock damaged her father beyond repair. Many years later Sarah would write in her diary, 'he grew old faster than his years and died at 60 . . . he was a kind, loving father.'

Sarah left home in adolescence and lived with relatives, making dresses in her spare time. Later she progressed to working for rich land owners, managing their servants and groundskeepers. It was not enough. She was never satisfied working for others and made plans to use the money she had saved to make and sell pretty dresses.

She never had the chance. As she prepared to go into business, her 'dear' sister Mary became sick. A doctor told her she would never be healthy in the north of England. So Mary, her husband John Carr, and their four-year-old son John junior sailed for the antipodes. Within months, Sarah received a letter from Mary, begging for her to come to Port Phillip. Weeks later she was on her way to the other side of the world.

There were some unsettling days aboard the *Rajah* but most were pleasing. Sarah took walks on the deck, looking up at the stars and down at the porpoises and flying fish. The trade winds went to work and in mid-November Captain Giles announced to his passengers they had arrived in Bass Strait. His final task was to steer them through Port Phillip's infamous gateway.

In the fifty-five years since the first white explorers had nudged their bows into the bay, The Heads had littered the seabed and coast with wrecks, cargo and men. The *Prince Albert*, a single-masted wooden cutter, carrying mail, wheat and maize from Sydney, had been the first to be smashed onto rocks by an awful wind in 1840. Searchers found one of four dead crewmen on a nearby beach beside two full mailbags. The *Thetis*, a two-masted schooner, was being sailed from Sydney to Melbourne – with cargo of iron, lead, wire, beer, tea, wine, timber and food – when it struck the outer reef and was tipped onto its side. The low tide allowed some passengers to climb to safety. Two children could not get a foothold and were washed away; their parents perished trying to find them.

It was well known that pirates had moved to the nearby coast, taking advantage of tragedy by plundering cargo from sinking boats, such was the lawlessness in parts of the new civilisation.

Not long before Sarah arrived aboard the *Rajah*, a ship carrying 382 emigrants, including 92 single women, arrived in Melbourne, having safely made it through The Heads. But it found trouble leaving the bay, slammed by a gale and large waves. The drunken captain ignored orders from an experienced pilot and sailed at the gap. His crewmen were no help; some of them had been locked in irons so they wouldn't abandon ship and dash for the goldfields. Six men in a whaleboat made a frantic rescue attempt as the ship broke apart on the rocks. The captain was last seen in a lifeboat calling for help and rum. Only ten of twenty-six crewmen survived. One of the rescuers also drowned. And the pirates moved in.

Captain Giles was no drunkard and the coastal thieves could only wonder at the contents of the *Rajah* as it waltzed through The Heads. Newspapers reported on 20 November 1855:

> Shipping Intelligence: Rajah of Sarawak, ship, 525 tons, Sheppard Giles, from Bristol . . . Passengers – Cabin: Mrs Kingsbury, Miss Jaggar (sic), Mr Sircom and family, Messrs. Watts (2), and five in the steerage.

That Sarah's name was misspelled mattered little. She would soon go by another, in her new life as leading citizen of a town being made in the image of the finest English fishing villages.

Three

Melbourne was having its strangest decade. The broad-street, foul-smelling city had become a porthole for gold diggers of all accents heading bush upon carts, horseback or by weary legs. The madness of the earliest rush years had eased by 1855 but the fever was yet unbroken. New finds were still drawing into the hills hopeful migrants, followed by tradesmen and merchants. Towns were growing in the north, west and east. The colony's population would increase from 76,000 to 540,000 by 1860.

Amid the port's mayhem, Sarah Jagger saw John Carr, her brother in law, and boarded his cart with her luggage, including a surprisingly large bundle of drapery. Mr Carr drove her south, away from the din, on hardly used roads and through sparse suburbs into the land of gum trees, passing only the odd commuter on a horse, gig or bullock-drawn drays. After a while, Sarah began to worry about the distance she had been taken from the city. Each turn of the wheels gave her a twist of anxiety and the relief at having completed her sea voyage was soon replaced by trepidation.

Where on earth are we going, she wondered. They were following the coast.

The bay of Port Phillip is the shape of a human head facing east; viewed on a map, Melbourne is at the crown and its southern suburbs are dotted along the forehead. The large city of Geelong lies away to the west. Sarah and Mr Carr were heading twenty-six miles down the face, where the eyes might be, to a place called Frankston.

If she were fearful of meeting trouble along the way, she didn't say anything, though it would have been understandable for any traveller to be wary. There had been crimes committed on this path. Melbourne residents knew of two recent bloody incidents: a double strangling murder four miles from Brighton Hotel, and a shooting by bushrangers. Both barbarous incidents led to hangings.

Two thirds of the way to Frankston, Sarah and Mr Carr reached a farming village called Mordialloc, boasting stables, a general store, a curving creek with no bridge and an unbroken view of the water. From here, the contours of the land changed from tall trees and grassland to white beaches, sand dunes and an enormous inland swamp teeming with kangaroos, emus and a million mud eels. The Boon Wurrung called the wetland Carrum Carrum. Sarah and Mr Carr might have called it a nuisance because there was no track through it. They had to ei ther go along the beach or head all the way around, a full day's trek. The beach route was faster and they took it. The sand was soft but packed tight along the low-tide mark.

Hours later they came to their destination, home to a dozen or so people in wattle and daub huts.

Frankston had been home to Europeans – missionaries and surveyors – since 1836; farmers with pastoral leases followed and eventually the government started selling land for a pound per acre.

Sarah had only been in town a short time when she met two Melbourne gentlemen on a shooting excursion. One of the men was the brother of someone she had known in Manchester. James 'J. B.' Thompson was a Cambridge graduate, who had travelled to Australia to work as a journalist. He was also a leading cricketer.

Mr Thompson surprised Sarah by offering her a job as his housekeeper back in the city. She declined. She would never again be a servant. The tired journeywoman only wanted to be close to her sister, who was just as ill as she had been in England. Sarah was shocked when she saw her sibling, looking 'so very altered . . . thin and old'. Despite her poor health, Mary was pregnant. She had the child and named her Sarah. But the infant died two months later.

The next year saw impressive development in Frankston. Sarah began working by the needle, sewing for decent pay anything new houses needed. Her life changed forever when the town bigwig Frank Liardet employed a well-regarded builder to make him a homestead on his large property Ballam Ballam.

The builder was Thomas Cogger Allchin, an ambitious Englishman from the county of Kent, whose broad eyebrows framed kind eyes.

Early in 1857 Thomas Allchin successfully proposed marriage to Sarah Jagger, or at least 'put in his claim for a wife'. She knew her fiancé had built the first hotel at a nearby place called Schnapper Point and thought he was in 'good circumstances'. After a short delay, Sarah and Thomas went all the way to the city and were wed by special licence in a church. They posed for a photograph that afternoon; Sarah did not smile but her husband hinted at one.

Sarah continued to live in Frankston. She wanted to move to Schnapper Point but her husband told her their new house was not finished, because thieves were pinching his timber and nails every time he was away on business. After several weeks she decided she was done waiting and would move, 'house or no house!'

Thomas, who was living at The Point, sent one of his employees aboard a dray to collect his bride from Frankston. Mary told Sarah a lady should never travel in such a way. But Sarah Allchin wanted to belong to a place that also belonged to her. She dressed in her best crinoline and smartest bonnet and tried to ignore the smell of the bullocks that towed her up and over a southern beachside hill called Oliver's. The track from Frankston to Schnapper Point was potholed but endurable. Between the two towns was a house upon a rise called Mount Eliza, whose cliffs rimmed the bay and extended all the way to her new residence. Sarah overlooked the stunning blue vista, a view she would take in every day for the rest of her life.

On arrival at Schnapper Point, Sarah saw a town just out of infancy. The public house her husband had built – Tanti Hotel – was the central meeting place of locals.

The government had been successful in selling most of the land surrounding the new township. A man called Alexander Balcombe had bought a large chunk of the peninsula. Balcombe had a measure of celebrity. His father, William, had been a British naval officer, who had settled on the island of St Helena in 1804 as a merchant for the East India Company. A decade later, the Emperor of the French, Napoleon Bonaparte, was held prisoner on the island after his defeat in the Battle of Waterloo. William Balcombe befriended Napoleon and hosted him at his house, The Briars. Their close bond led to Balcombe's dismissal and relocation to London, although he was never charged with a crime and was eventually given a reprieve, posted to Australia as Colonial Treasurer of New South Wales, where he died within five years. His children were awarded land for their father's service. Alexander, educated at Sydney Grammar School, chose Port Phillip.

The Point wasn't perfect for farming but the earth was full of useful clay, and it grew she-oak, which was logged and hauled in boats to Melbourne to be used as railway sleepers. (Thomas Allchin took advantage of this. He was a timber merchant, as well as a builder.) English fruit trees were starting to flourish in new gardens. And the bay was full of catch. For years to come, residents would boast to visitors they were living in the district most 'likely to become the Ramsgate of Victoria', akin to one of the most glamorous seaside towns in Britain.

Thomas was waiting for Sarah inside their unfinished house. It had no curtains, no proper furniture, not even a door. Sarah dismounted the dray and rushed to inspect the two rooms, noting humble contents: an old sofa frame, three bottomless chairs, a table (one leg smashed), two small saucepans and a teakettle. There was a stash of crockery, bought from a man who had previously rented the shell of a house. Sarah could not hide her dismay.

But at least they could eat well. The Allchins' first hometown meal was a schnapper that had been swimming in the bay earlier that day. On first tasting, they knew why Balcombe had chosen it for the town's title. On full stomachs the couple unpacked Sarah's belongings, covered the windows with some material, propped up the unhung door with boxes, spread her bedding on the floor and went to sleep. The next morning Sarah awoke to find the bullocks had eaten the precious material she had hauled all the way from England.

Thomas went away on business the same day and Sarah tried to make their house a home, first creating ottomans from the boxes, covering them tastefully. This was a pattern repeated for months: Thomas travelled and Sarah continued improving their standard of living, just as her neighbours were doing throughout the township.

With progress came hardship for all those residents, including Sarah and Thomas Allchin. In 1858 they had their first child. Seven days later the baby died and was buried at the new cemetery. The parents went back to work.

Sarah later wrote about her life in papers that have been passed down through the Allchin family. She called her life 'an uneventful one, woven for me by a kind of providence'. Her strong faith sustained her. She was also being modest. No guiding hand held hers when she sailed in the mid-nineteenth century without friends or family from Bristol to Melbourne. No fortune was gifted her on arrival at her new ramshackle accommodation. The cause of her success was her unbreakable will, a shining example to all, including the four more children she and Thomas would watch grow into adulthood.

Four

Life at The Point, as with most communities in colonial Australia, was consumed by work, with Saturday afternoon for washing up and only Sunday for rest. But people can't work all the time and stay youthful or contented. There has to be *more* to living. And as Sarah and Thomas Allchin worked alongside the Balcombes and other townsfolk to build a community with a jetty, post office, churches, schools and boarding houses, a new sporting movement was beginning in Melbourne that would eventually transform all their lives.

Up until the end of the fifties, non-working-class men played games with and against each other when they could in summer. Cricket was well established; hunting was a prominent 'sport'; gambling on horseracing was also popular. But there was little or nothing to do on Saturday afternoons when autumn drained the colour from the sky and gave in to winter. Depressing weather cannot quell the natural yearning for fun. So, in 1858, some prominent – and bored – men gathered in a city pub to invent a new style of football.

They reasoned it was a game to keep cricketers fit while their fields were too wet. But from the first match, Australian football would mean more to its followers than its intention; played well it would be an unprecedented harmonious marriage of violence and passion, celebrated in equal measure by men and women.

Sport had been part of Australian life for centuries. Indigenous children played games like *murri murri* (throwing spears at bark), *bubberah* (boomerang-throwing), and *marn grook* (kicking opossum skins). The birthdate of organised sport for white Australians was October 1810, when Governor Lachlan Macquarie told the 73rd Regiment to clear some ground for a racetrack in Sydney. Gambling had already become one of the colony's downtime fancies, so horses had been raced against each other for wagers by this time. Macquarie agreed to something more formal, giving permission for a three-day carnival on the land that would one day be Hyde Park. He wrote to the public warning against 'all species of Gaming, Drunkenness, Swearing, Quarrelling, Fighting or Boxing taking place on or near the Race Ground!'

There were other sports in Australia to fill the time before team games started up. In Sydney, pugilists went at each other bare-fisted under the Broughton Rules (Jack Broughton was the father of English boxing) of 1743. Some matches lasted hours and ended only when someone was knocked out. Outsiders have always criticised the barbarism of boxing. Devotees call it a sport of honour and courage and skill. Either way, it is hard for most people to love watching fists repeatedly thumping heads. Australia's growing public needed something else to cheer about in their little time away from making a living.

Just three years after the founding of Melbourne, in the final weeks of spring 1838, five gentlemen had signed a document that gave birth to the Melbourne Cricket Club. Subscription cost a guinea. The first match was on the site of the future Royal Mint in William Street. *The Port Phillip Gazette* reported, 'Did we not witness the gentlemen of the district assemble last Saturday week on the beautiful pleasure grounds around the fast rising town, to bring into practice one of the most elegant and manly sports that can be imagined?'

Teams were cobbled together in many forms: the MCC versus the Melbourne Union Cricket Club, gentlemen against tradesmen, military and civilians, even 'whiskers' versus 'clean shaven'.

Some colonial football had been played in the 1840s, but detailed reports of those games didn't make it into print so records of style don't exist. Picnic sports meetings were held on public holidays and at least one newspaper noted there would be a 'Grand Match at the old English Game of Football'.

Two teams played a twelve-a-side football match the following year to celebrate the separation of New South Wales and the Port Phillip settlement. Esteemed historian Geoffrey Blainey contended the 'tussles must have followed a variety of rules, some of which were home-made'.

In July 1858, Tom Wills, one of the founders of the football code known today as Australian rules, wrote his famous letter to *Bell's Life*, calling for regular winter games:

> Now that cricket has been put aside for some few months to come, and cricketers have assumed somewhat of the chrysalis nature . . . rather than allow this state of torpor to creep over them, and stifle their new supple limbs, why can they not, I say, form a foot-ball club.

Wills was born on a sheep run in New South Wales and educated in England. He had returned to Melbourne to be one of its finest cricketers. Biographer Greg de Moore (*Tom Wills: His Spectacular Rise and Tragic Fall*) called Wills a 'rapscallion for the ages . . . not beholden to the conventions of the day', whose 'foot-ball' suggestion was inspired by his experience playing rugby overseas.

Wills' call for football was heard and several unofficial, rugby-style matches were played in parklands before a proper match was scheduled between Scotch College and Melbourne Grammar. The Melbourne Cricket Ground was not made available, so the game was played in the nearby grass, in between the trees. Wills recommended an oval-shaped ball be used but the schools preferred a round one.

It was 7 August 1858. The winner was the first team to score two goals. But there were forty people on each side – thirty-seven boys and three masters for Melbourne Grammar and thirty-six boys and four masters for Scotch – and the field was half a mile long, so it was hard to score. The game went for five hours on the first day, both teams scoring once. A *Morning Herald* scribe wrote, 'most jubilant were the cheers that rang among the gum-trees and she-oaks'. Play resumed a fortnight later and again a week after that. Eventually the contest was declared a draw. Far from being an anticlimax, the game proved to be the sport's foundation stone.

A year later Tom Wills and three other fellows co-founded the Melbourne Football Club and sat together at the Parade Hotel in East Melbourne to codify their new game. The other rule makers were public school teacher Thomas Smith, journalist William Hammersley and another writer, J. B. Thompson – the same man who had tried in vain to employ Sarah Allchin at their meeting in Frankston. The gentlemen made a document outlining the field distance (to be decided upon by opposing captains), the kick-off to start the match, goals ('fairly between the posts, without touching either of them'), the behind (a missed goal attempt), the mark (a catch), and rough play. Tripping and pushing were allowed. 'Hacking' of a player in 'rapid motion' was banned.

And the ball could never be thrown.

It became obvious within months the rules were open to change. Another committee meeting was held at the Parade Hotel a month later. J. B. Thompson moved a motion to ban tripping and holding, as well as hacking; he also proposed a 'free kick' rule, which remains today.

The earliest custodians of the game could not have envisaged the effect their meetings would have on Australia. The allure of football would spread, slowly at first, from the city in all directions, to towns like Schnapper Point and beyond. It was a gift to all those children born in the sixties and seventies, no matter their class. Saturday afternoon games, once the domain of the rich and self-employed, would belong to all.

Five

Every morning James and Jane Caldwell awoke to sounds of their son, Willie, fighting his lungs for air; daybreak after daybreak they rushed to see him sitting up in bed, his skin pale blue, a deep cough, like a baby seal's bark, shaking his tiny frame with each repetition. His mother and father had to wonder whether the toddler might soon die from one of these fits.

In 1874, the Caldwell family lived in the gold-mining town of Maryborough in central Victoria. James and Jane had four children – Willie was their youngest. It had been a year since the malady seized him. His parents knew he should have improved by now because the others – Alice, Tom and Jim – had shaken off their woes within months.

The advice of a local doctor was that Willie might breathe easier in another town, away from those dry, dusty tracks and paddocks. James, a Presbyterian minister, told Jane he would ask the church if it had another posting for him. He sent a request to Melbourne headquarters by Cobb and Co. mail. The Caldwells, who did not come from country Victoria and were not emotional about the place, waited to find out where life would next take them.

And they prayed Willie would not suffocate in his sleep.

Reverend James Caldwell was born in 1825 at a Northern Irish village called Antrim, best known as the 1798 battleground for warring British soldiers and Irish insurgents. He was a smart lad and went on to study religion in Belfast. On 17 August 1859, Rev. Caldwell married his first wife, Lizzie Long, at St Mary's in Dublin. The newlyweds decided they wanted to raise a family in a nation with brighter promise. They sailed from Liverpool to Melbourne, where Rev. Caldwell was given stewardship – or 'inducted to the charge' – of a temporary church in East Collingwood, one of the city's poorest suburbs. The population was still in boom and Rev. Caldwell soon discovered it would increase by one – Lizzie was pregnant. In the winter of 1860 the couple had a daughter, Elizabeth, who would not live to see summer. *The Age* newspaper ran a note on 21 November 1860:

> DIED. On the 18th November, at 81 Gore Street, Collingwood, Elizabeth Long, infant daughter of the Rev. James Caldwell.

Within months, Lizzie died, too. Typhoid killed her.

Rev. Caldwell did not return to Ireland to grieve. He continued to work. For the next year he oversaw construction of the bluestone St George's Presbyterian Church. Its foundation stone was laid two days before Christmas in 1861.

Five years later, Rev. Caldwell decided he wanted to marry again after meeting a kind and caring Tasmanian called Jane Lindsay. Jane was the fifth daughter of the late William Lindsay, a rich ticket-of-leave merchant from Hobart Town. How they came to know each other was not recorded in any surviving family documents. It is possible the minister had crossed Bass Strait on church business. It was common during those years for clergymen to gather at intercolonial conferences, a practice made formal by 'Federal Assemblies' from the 1880s.

Hobart Town hosted the Caldwell-Lindsay wedding on 24 May 1866 at St John's in Macquarie Street. The *Tasmanian Morning Herald* recorded that the ceremony was performed by two of the groom's colleagues – Rev. J. Service and Rev. C. Simpson.

Jane was twenty-two, almost half her husband's age. She moved to live with Rev. Caldwell in Melbourne and soon gave birth to a daughter named Alice in November 1867. Two years later the family sailed to visit Rev. Caldwell's relatives in Ireland, where Jane had a son, Thomas. On returning to Melbourne, the family bought – with money from Jane's inheritance – a row of three two-storey houses in Gipps Street, East Melbourne. The stylish, modern building would have made a comfortable home for the parents and their two children, but Rev. Caldwell had agreed to take on a job in the bush.

Within a year of wheeling into Maryborough, Jane had

another son – named James but more often called Jim. Then came William, named after his maternal grandfather.

Two whooping-cough epidemics in four years did not prevent the family of six having some fun at the family manse. Rev. Caldwell regularly hosted his brother ministers. With fondness, his children would later remember the Rev. Henry Finlay popping in from neighbouring Dunolly. Rev. Finlay had been at college with Rev. Caldwell in Belfast. He liked the kids, especially Jim.

'Well, Jim,' he said one day. 'God Almighty had given you a beautiful face, and I hope you will make good use of it.'

Jim was the handsomest Caldwell because of his flawless features and arching eyelashes. But Willie was the cutest. He had a flat nose that made his laughter musical. A lady visitor to the Maryborough home once said Willie's chuckle was, 'just like a silver bell, going up and down a scale'. Alice and Tom, the older children, were more serious than Jim and Willie. Even as youngsters, their lot was to help their parents as much as they could.

Rev. Caldwell was a man of respect in Maryborough. His short career in that town was recognised by the *Jubilee History of the Presbyterian Church, Maryborough*, which recalled:

> Much good work was done during this time, and there is no doubt but that the church considerably benefitted by the efforts of this rev. gentleman. He was exceedingly popular, and his genial manner endeared him to all with whom he came in contact. The Rev. Mr Caldwell preached his farewell sermon on March 15th, 1874.

Church administrators searched the colony for Rev. Caldwell's next challenge, made necessary by little Willie's poor health and the doctor's advice. There were no vacancies in established suburbs or big towns. His only hope was in emerging villages. Eventually, they found one.

The Caldwells packed up their belongings and drove a horse-drawn carriage hundreds of kilometres back into Melbourne and down the face of Port Phillip to a green and blue beachside paradise previously called Schnapper Point, by now renamed Mornington – after the Earl of Mornington, Marquis Wellesley, a former Governor-General of India.

It was the sweetest time of year to arrive. The foreshore ti-tree was covered in white flowers, as if snow had just fallen on them, and English-like gardens were delightful. Mansions had been built on the hilltops overlooking the neat-as-a-hedge Main Street, which was populated by storekeepers, farmers, carters, brickmakers, a shoemaker, farrier, schoolmaster, victualler, saddler, seamstress, solicitor, butchers and fishermen.

The town's first full-time Presbyterian minister and his family breathed the clean salt air and sensed they had arrived in a special place they would never want to leave. No home was available to them initially so they lived for a spell in the Melbourne postmaster's holiday residence, where Jane gave birth to another son, Hugh.

So began the family's brightest decade.

Six

Willie touched his mother's side and made her look down at his tubby face.

'Mamma, I 'ave an owl in my pocket,' he said.

'What?' Jane asked.

'An owl.'

He pointed to his chest; Alice, Tom, Jim and the family's housekeeper stopped what they were doing and took an interest in his claim.

Jane inspected his jacket. 'No, Willie,' she said. 'There is nothing in your pocket, dear.'

'Yes, there is an OWL,' said Willie, who had a bright, healthy face and no longer coughed in the mornings. 'And I can't keep anything in. Everything falls out, because there is an owl in my pocket.'

Jane was suppressing a laugh when Rev. Caldwell came into the room to see what had upset Willie. The minister tried to locate the owl but could only find a finger-sized hole. Smiling, he told Willie they would fix it. It would be okay.

The presence of the bonny baby Hugh caused another beam of joy in the household; from his birth, family and visitors described him as ruddy, strong and hearty. He was a gifted kid. From the time he first walked, he wanted to run. His only problem was he expected too much from his legs and often tumbled forward trying to sprint everywhere. It seemed to harden him, good preparation for growing up with three older brothers.

Hugh did what he needed to be included in every sibling activity. Tom, Jim and Willie liked to wrestle on the front lawn. Hugh always joined in and went as hard as anyone until injury inevitably halted the battle. If he screamed or yelped, his brothers would stop and watch to see if he would cry, worried they might be in trouble for hurting Mumma's favourite. But he rarely showed distress.

'It is better now,' Hugh would say, standing up, relaxing Tom, Jim and Willie.

'It is better now, Mumma . . .' he would shout if Jane rushed over.

Tom was Hugh's hero. When the eldest boy wet his hair to make it curl, so did the youngest, forever patting down his brown mop with a wet brush.

'Is it nearly curly now, Mumma?' Hugh said, water dripping into his eyes. 'Yes, Hughie, darling,' she said. 'Nearly.'

More patting.

The Caldwells bought a large property and built a big house with a perfect bay's view a block away from Main Street. The red-bricked, two-storey, eleven-roomed manse was a home as grand as any in the district. Real-estate agents called it a commodious dwelling. It had brick stabling, with a washhouse and other outbuildings. Rev. Caldwell used his wife's money to fund construction.

It was rare for preachers to live in such lavish homes but Rev. Caldwell had unusually fine taste. The house – called Glen Bank – was surrounded by up to a dozen acres of land that would become an orchard. Sounds of a flowing creek named Tanti could be heard from almost anywhere on the Caldwell property; it carried rushes of water that had fallen in the mountains to the east and was always full of fish.

The Caldwells had several servants. One was a maintenance man, known to the children only as Johnston. Willie liked him best. When Johnston went to the stables for his midday meal, Willie liked to follow, though his mother didn't approve. If Johnston heard Jane Caldwell warning her son to stay away, he hollered back, 'He's no bother at all.'

This only became a problem when Rev. Caldwell found out Willie had been eating some of Johnston's food. 'Now, Willie,' he said. 'I know a little boy who, I think, ate some of Johnston's dinner, and I think he ought to take some of this nice pudding in return.'

Willie did not blush. It gave him a chance to visit the stables again. 'I'll take it to Johnston meself.'

None of the Caldwell children had problems making friends. When it came time to go to school, they skipped to it.

Rev. Caldwell left most of the parenting to Jane and their employees. As the only Presbyterian minister in the district, he had much to do. After he held his first service in Mornington, parishioners praised him for a week.

The Irishman was an impressive orator with a knack for choosing the right passages and tone. Preparation was his secret. He would spend all Fridays and Saturdays writing and rewriting his sermons, a ritual he would keep for the next twenty-eight years.

The history of organised religion at The Point had been brief. In the 1850s, half the town's residents had belonged to the Church of England. The first chapel was St Peter's, built in 1860 by a highly regarded builder, William Grover. Part-time ministers came every week from Melbourne by the steamers that were ferrying people and goods across the bay.

During these early years, the Presbyterians gathered on the Sabbath at the rear of a general store. In the 1860s some wealthy men, including holiday-house owner Scotch College principal Dr Alexander Morrison, donated money to construct a Gothic-style church in the town's centre. In February 1867, *The Argus* reported Mornington's first church tea meeting:

> Upward of 200 persons were entertained. This pretty church, a portion only of which is at present completed, will form an ornament . . . its site being one of the best in the locality.

The church's bricks were the same colour as the Caldwells' manse. In fact, all the bricks in town looked similar. They came from the same clay hole, owned by a prominent businessman and his wife: Thomas and Sarah Allchin.

The Allchins had spent the previous sixteen years making a fortune. Thomas had continued travelling the countryside chasing business deals. For a long time he employed axe men to fell trees he transported to Melbourne. To save on bullock and driver costs, he bought a small boat – known as a ketch – called *Governor La Trobe*. The vessel was constantly sailing wood to the city. Money and rations he made from this went into a general store the Allchins had opened in Main Street. The store sold everything from tobacco and hardware to the splendid English needlework Sarah was making after hours.

Some of Thomas' business deals flopped, causing marital angst. Half the time his wife didn't know what he was up to. She suspected he was managing a store or two in other towns and perhaps not paying his workers. Menacing men visited Sarah's front door, chasing up her husband's debts. But, as with most successful partnerships, the Allchins came to complement each other. Thomas remained industrious and ambitious. His clay pit was a lasting success and, though he had lost some of his profits on other speculations, hard-working Sarah squandered nothing. Even during her pregnancies, she worked up to eighteen hours a day to make the general store the best on the peninsula.

The biggest boon for the Allchins was the growth of the town. Cobb and Co. had started running a four-horse and carriage service between Mornington and the city, leaving at dawn, returning in the afternoon. There were two sizes of Cobb and Co. coaches, one able to carry eight passengers and the other fourteen. Travel in this way was expensive; a single fare to Melbourne cost two-thirds the weekly wage of a labourer. Sarah often rode the coach to Melbourne to buy drapery and other stores. She bought her flour from a gentleman called Thomas Thompson (brother of James, the footballer, cricketer and journalist), who she had known in Manchester. One day, she tried to buy three bags but Thompson told her to buy a ton. She told him she didn't have enough money.

'Never mind, pay me next time,' he said, explaining that there were going to be changes in the industry that would increase the price of flour. Sarah stood to make many times her usual profit.

It turned out to be yet another windfall for the Allchins. Land purchases followed. Thomas and Sarah paid eighty-nine pounds to extend their store. Then they bought another building on a corner lot and rented it to the Oriental Bank (later the Colonial). They bought another six acres of towering she-oaks upon which they wanted to build their dream home, where they could raise their children Emmie, Tom, Ella and baby Charlie.

These beachside acres were prime and the Allchins made their house big enough to be called a mansion, with a tower overlooking vessels coming and going from the harbour.

In the few hours a week they weren't working, Thomas and Sarah walked with their kids through the village and foreshore, enjoying their neighbours' greetings and looking forward to the next formal social gatherings, another feature of their growing community.

'A pretty little watering place,' is how Melburnians first described Mornington. But by the mid-1870s it had become something grander. City dwellers came by sail or steam between October and April for relief from the heat.

Travel writers tried to capture the spirit of the coast. 'A desirable retreat,' wrote one visiting scribe. 'As yet these seaside villages have not much accommodation to boast of, and have no attractions in the way of gaiety to offer, even German bands being a rarity; but probably before many years have passed they may be . . . enlivened by minstrels and marionettes.'

Each passing year brought progress. New veranda-post shops and public buildings went up each summer. Leading townsfolk made decisions about employing bullock teams to grub tree stumps to clear land for more streets, though drays always seemed to be sticking in wheel-deep sand or mud. Horse-drawn rollers were used to compress thoroughfares and workmen filled potholes with gravel sourced from foreshore cliffs whenever they threatened harm.

After a big rain the gravel-topped roads glowed a shade of red and their puddles appeared orange in low light. Against the greener grass and bluer water, the colours of Mornington were, at times, almost fantastic.

The early settlers, always determined to preserve natural beauty, made important town-planning decisions that future generations would always appreciate. The most significant was to clear and keep a vast park near the beach. Local government decided, 'On no account were licences be issued for removal of gravel from the area set aside in perpetuity for recreational purposes.'

The brightest flower of the district – Mornington Park – bloomed year round as a stage for picnics, music and sport. It was here, on this slanting field, that the children of the Caldwells and Allchins – and all the other local families – came to know each other intimately enough to make lifelong bonds.

Seven

Skinny Charlie Allchin and the rugged Caldwell boys, who lived less than half a mile apart, were mates from the moment they were introduced, and most of their adventures, even before they were old enough to go to school, involved exploring the Australian bush and beach.

The Caldwells owned a changing shed on the sand and used it as their headquarters every summer. Swimming restrictions were in place for the town's adults; men and women were required by law to bathe at different times. But the little ones could splash around in the shallows all day.

The most popular stretch was Mothers' Beach, named after all the nervous mothers standing at the water's edge, shouting to their children, 'Get ya head wet'; residents later recalled it was common knowledge at the time that if you stood in the sea without wetting your hair, you would soon die.

The baths, operated by leading citizen William Irvine, were the best place to wash off everything but salt from the water itself. Irvine was busiest during low tide, when the bay fell away and adults and children went cockle-hunting.

When there were no more cockles to be found, Charlie Allchin and the Caldwells chased tiny fish hour after long hour. In the harbour lived schools of silver fingerlings, always coming close to land and darting around the feet of waders. Camouflaged against the corrugated, golden seabed, the bullet-shaped species teased their laughing, short-legged pursuers, who kept track of the fish by watching their shadows, made by a sun that was slowly baking their skin and bleaching their hair. In the earliest years of their lives, only Sunday school drew them away from their favourite playground.

Charlie, Willie and Hugh always sat together in church. The Allchins were Wesleyan and had no church building or minister, so they prayed at St Andrew's and listened to Rev. Caldwell. All the boys loved signing. Their favourite hymn was *Golden Shore*:

We are out on the ocean sailing,
Homeward bound we sweetly glide;
We are out on the ocean sailing,
To a home beyond the tide.

Charlie and Willie, who were the same age, always smiled at each other while catching breath between verses.

Millions now are safely landed,
Over on the golden shore;
Millions more are on their journey,
Yet there's room for millions more.

Hugh, two years younger than Charlie and Willie, copied the older ones and almost shouted so his voice could be heard.

All the storms will soon be over,
Then we'll anchor in the harbour,
We are out on the ocean sailing,
To a home beyond the tide.

When the children weren't on song, they were restless. Intuitively, Rev. Caldwell was wary of his offspring disrupting his performance, so he offered inducements for them to stay quiet and still. Pudding was the most common reward. Little Hugh *loved* pudding but he was also a world-class wriggler. He once made too many movements and attracted his papa's cold stare. The boy winced and started to rub his eyes.

'Now I won't get any puddle,' he was heard to say.

But Hugh never missed out on pudding. His mother would not deny him. When another parishioner once told Jane Hughie was spoilt by sweets, she replied, 'You could not spoil Hughie . . . he is too good and contented; besides he is such a manly, independent little fellow.'

And the lad showed all of his independence the day he first went swimming out of his depth. Two of the family's servants, a nurse and maid, took Alice and her brothers to the beach for a quick bathe. Tom, Jim and the maid went in first, leaving Willie and Hugh sitting at the entrance of their family changing shed. Next, Alice, Hugh and the nurse took their turn. Some delinquents from town came by and began teasing the Caldwell children on the beach by stealing their shoes and socks. The nurse stormed out of the bay, her long dress dripping, to confront the pests, demanding they return the footwear. Everyone was watching the confrontation and no one saw Hugh, who was still in the water, walking into the deep, beyond his own height.

Alice spun to see where he was.

'Look at Hughie!' she yelled.

The toddler could no longer stand up but he was not panicking; rather, he was floating and laughing and splashing about. The nurse ran back in, up to her neck, and reached for Hughie, who was drifting like a stout tug, bobbing over the ripples. Alice was hysterical and had to be calmed.

Perils of the wilderness were revealed to all Mornington people in the 1870s, with several tragedies causing public anguish. The first involved two brothers dying at sea. Their names were Rudolph and Arthur Kirk, aged six and eight.

The Kirk boys went missing on 20 November 1875. Their mother had sent them to play in a paddock and became frightened when she did not hear from them by nightfall. Their father gathered a search party that combed nearby bushland all evening and throughout the night, hoping the boys had only lost their way.

Nothing.

Next morning, Mr Kirk found children's footmarks at the beach. A boat had been reported missing from the same spot. Two neighbourhood girls later told Mr Kirk they had seen his sons 'turning the boat around' before sunset. Soon more witnesses came forward; fishermen had seen the boat with two people in it, but although they thought it strange 'took no notice' – and did not mention it when they reached their homes.

The next day was spent in search. The entire community joined in: a fleet of boats launched; men and women lined the cliffs.

A fisherman called John Davis found the boat in chest-deep water fifteen miles north of Mornington. Davis waded in and looked in the hull. Rudolph was lying inside. He was dead in seven inches of water. Davis told a subsequent coronial inquiry, 'The deceased had taken off one boot and his trousers, and the latter were missing, but the boot was in the boat with his glengarry cap.'

A jury found the child had died by drowning, 'accelerated by cold and exposure'. Arthur was never found, though his cap was recovered from the bay and a false sighting of him was reported. Several hours after Rudolph was brought to shore, a woman claimed she saw the body of his older brother in the harbour at The Point. A fisherman named Mr Sears tried to walk into the water to look but became nervous and went no further. Another man, David Davies, who was an employer of the well-known hotelier Thomas Rennison, threw off his coat and swam out, revealing that the object was only seaweed. On his way back to land, Davies panicked and fell under the surface. Sears rushed back into the bay and dragged Davies out. But he was dead.

A newspaper story syndicated throughout the nation read, in part: 'How long the poor child [Rudolph] endured the pain and terror of such a night before his sufferings were terminated by death no one will ever know, but considering the state of the weather, life could scarcely have been long sustained. The distressing affair has occasioned the greatest excitement at Schnapper Point, and the parents of the unfortunate children are the objects of universal sympathy.'

The bay may be noble but it never forgave mistakes.

About the time of the Kirk tragedy, talk in Main Street turned to a double murder, involving a Mornington hotelier. Henry Howard had a quarrel with his girlfriend, Elizabeth Wright, who ran a pub in Frankston and was having an affair with her barman. The local newspaper *South Bourke and Mornington Journal* told that Howard found the two together and 'stabbed Wright four times in the heart with a large butcher's knife, causing instantaneous death'. Howard then rammed the knife into the barman's chest, leaving the victims lying together in their blood. For this, he was hanged in Melbourne Gaol.

There were worse tragedies.

In 1877, major Melbourne newspapers reported the death of a man called Jimmy Dunbar under the headline: 'Last of the Boon wurrung'.

In his final years, Dunbar had been recognisable throughout the district for his boomerang skill and wit. An artist drew a colour picture of him in 1870. He was sitting inside his parkland hut under a blue shawl that looked like a cape. He wore a thick, rounded beard and an expression of concern; or was it annoyance?

Seven skinny dogs stood and sat at his feet.

In hindsight, it was clear the Boon Wurrung was doomed from the arrival of those first European sealers and whalers, who brought disease and violence. The Indigenous people's demise had been further accelerated by white settlement. As local historian Leo Gamble wrote, 'There was a terrible inevitability about what happened between blacks and whites during the nineteenth century in the Port Phillip district.'

When the tribes of the Kulin nation began suffering in the years after Batman's treaty, the British Government created the position of Protector of Aborigines. The job was given to George Augustus Robinson, who'd been a mediator between settlers and tribes in Van Diemen's Land. Under Robinson's watch, the protectorate was a failure but one of its rare successes was the appointment of William Thomas as welfare agent for the Boon Wurrung. Thomas counted the Boon Wurrung population at 83 in 1839, probably an underestimate but still alarmingly low. From then he lived and worked among the survivors. He wrote in his diaries about the last stages of the Boon Wurrung's natural existence, how the tribesmen and women moved with the seasons, made weapons from the trees and bags or nets from the tussock grass.

'All are employed,' Thomas noted. 'Children in getting gum, knocking down birds . . . women in digging up roots, killing bandicoots, getting grubs . . . the men in hunting kangaroos . . . scaling trees for opossums . . .'

This life was made impossible after the arrival of the first squatters. Disease, rum and murder took the lives of more and more of the land's real owners. Although tribal descendants would survive among future generations, by the 1870s there were fewer than ten original Boon Wurrung alive. They lived near Mordialloc, catching eels in Carrum Carrum swamp, selling them to the white farmers and dray travellers.

One by one they succumbed to fatal illness, until only Jimmy Dunbar and his wife, Nancy, remained.

The Dunbars died a week apart. Jimmy's dogs did not believe he was gone and followed his hearse all the way to the Alfred Hospital in Melbourne, refusing to leave the street outside the building for a long time.

For the next two decades the older residents of Mornington and surrounding towns could remember, with increasing fondness, the evenings they used to spend listening to the corroborees just outside their townships. They told their children about them and those young ones – such as Charlie and the Caldwells – went looking for the old tracks and campsites, which were still there. Like the Boon Wurrung before them, the first white Australian natives would follow well-made bush paths to hunt; at night they would sit around freshly lit flames and look up at the Southern Cross; and after dinner they would sing and smoke and play their instruments until sleep induced them to dreaming.

Eight

Jim was six, Willie four and Hugh two when their mother went into labour again. Though she was anxious, Jane Caldwell was thankful she was having her sixth baby delivered in Mornington. The worst place to be born was Melbourne; its infant mortality rate was higher than London. Until fitted with sewerage in 1897, 'Smellbourne', as it was nicknamed, was an open toilet with regularly polluted water. The most prolific killer during the early settlement decades was colonial fever, properly diagnosed by the 1870s as typhoid.

Mornington people sometimes complained about their sanitation. British-born residents never got used to outdoor toilets – 'earth closets' – but most were dignified about their situation. 'One gets used to the odd smell or two,' was the general thinking.

Jane had her fifth son in 1877 and called him Ernest John Caldwell. Geography did not save him. He died within months.

The grieving mother was never the same.

Jane Caldwell was a loving and affectionate woman, who suffered bouts of depression. Her daughter Alice once described her mumma as naturally delicate. She was also lonely. Although Jane had her children for company, Rev. Caldwell was often travelling for work. As the years fell away, her sadness became more burdensome.

The Caldwells had three more children. Two years after Ernest died, Jane had her second daughter, named Jane but called Jeannie; a year later she gave birth to her sixth son, named John but always known as Jack. In 1881, the family celebrated the safe arrival of another girl, Sarah, who answered to Sallie. In the Glen Bank house, Jeannie, Jack and Sallie would always be referred to as 'the little ones'.

By the time her youngest was two, Jane could barely keep up with her eight children. The eldest, Tom, was old enough now to be considered a young adult. The rest were in a hurry to catch him. Days were jammed with games, quarrels, school, church, and no quiet time.

Parents can only cope with mayhem if they sleep well at night. And Jane was not sleeping at all. In April 1883, she decided she could not stay in Mornington any longer. She wanted to move to the city, or least be somewhere else. Rev. Caldwell arranged temporary accommodation for his wife with a colleague in Melbourne and sent word to a doctor that Jane needed help.

Next weekend the couple walked down to the jetty and caught a steamer to the city. They landed at Sandridge (soon to be renamed Port Melbourne) and strolled to Hobson's Bay railway station. The Sandridge to Melbourne line was just two and a half miles long but Rev. Caldwell would not ride with Jane the rest of the way. He saw her onto a carriage and they said goodbye. Ten minutes later the mother of eight and her luggage rolled into the busy, two-platform Melbourne Terminus (now Flinders Street station). Greeting her on arrival was her husband's mate, Presbyterian minister Duncan McEachran. The minister flagged a cab and rode with Jane to his home in Carlton, where he lived with his wife.

Rev. McEachran was a leading Victorian church stalwart. In his late fifties, with a broad Scottish accent, he led the largest congregation in the city, up from 120 to 800 since he'd taken over in 1868. He was said to be an eloquent and fervent preacher, a promoter of daily prayer and Bible study. He was held in high esteem by other ministers, including Rev. James Caldwell. Five years earlier, Rev. McEachran had stayed in Mornington while on an evangelical tour of the colony. Jane's stay at the Carlton manse was terrible. A doctor visited her several times but could not ease her sense of hopelessness. Without family nearby, she felt worse than before. Increasingly, she thought about dying. She was thirty-nine years old.

Jane had been born into a rich and happy family. Her father, William Lindsay, was an Englishman who was transported to Van Diemen's Land for possessing counterfeit money. He was sentenced to fourteen years but good behaviour cut his term to two years and nine months. Thereafter, he became a liquor merchant, hotelier and prolific land buyer, who had eight children with two wives. When William Lindsay died after accidentally drinking poison in 1862, his funeral was attended by members of parliament. The Premier called him 'the most upright and honourable man I knew'. He left his fifty-thousand-pound fortune to his children.

Jane Lindsay was seventeen when she attended her father's wake. Within five years she was married to Rev. James Caldwell, though she never broke her bond with Tasmania. Two of her sisters married into the equally wealthy Field family on pristine country near Launceston. In years to come the Fields would be close to Jane's children, particularly Tom and Jim.

The morning of 10 April 1883 was flat and grey and rainy. Newspapers landing on doorsteps had nothing much to tell: there was a Chinese gold-mining protest; an accident in the city had left a man in hospital with a broken leg; a twelve-year-old boy had been hurt falling in a puddle on Little Lonsdale Street.

Jane Caldwell had been living under the watch of Rev. McEachran and his wife for six days. At 10 am she heard a visitor knock at the front door. It was a woman named Letitia Haywood. She lived in nearby Fitzroy and had come to see if Jane was okay. Letitia and Jane had been friends, or at least acquaintances, for three or four years. It is not certain how they met but it was probably through the church. Letitia had been to the house four or five times in as many days.

Jane's face was a mirror of the sky. She had not improved since Rev. Caldwell said goodbye to her at the railway station the previous Wednesday. She told Letitia, 'I will never get right,' and warned, 'I will make away with myself.'

Over the next three hours Letitia failed to drag Jane toward reason. Jane told Letitia to go away. Eventually, she did.

Jane told Mrs McEachran she was going for a short walk.

She carried an umbrella, as anyone would that dull afternoon. Rev. McEachran came home to learn that Jane had gone out and not returned. He found Letitia to ask her about her visit but was not told about the threat of suicide. Letitia could not bring herself to repeat it.

Night came, then another day. Jane had not come back.

Rev. McEachran sent news of Jane's disappearance to Mornington. Rev. Caldwell rushed to Melbourne to lead the search. A grim week went by without any sightings, although her hat and umbrella were found near the Yarra River. Notices went up, appealing for help finding her.

About 9 am the following Tuesday, a man named Septimus Gadenne, a local writer, was walking beside the Yarra near the Johnston Street Bridge when he saw a floating body. He did not know Jane Caldwell but had heard she was missing. He waded in, dragged the corpse to land and then ran to the Collingwood police station to tell what he had found. Constable Daniel Coakley went back to the riverbank with Gadenne and together the men carried Jane to the Early Bird Hotel, a single-storey brick building in front of the local brewery, just a few hundred yards away.

Rev. Caldwell was nearby. The clergyman came to the pub as soon as he could and watched as Constable Coakley examined his wife's body. The policeman found some money in a pocket but nothing else. She was wearing all her rings.

The policeman made some notes in rushed, sloping handwriting. They read: 'There were no signs of any struggle having preceded death. There were no marks or injury that I could see. The body was in the water I should say seven or eight days.'

The Argus newspaper published the discovery the next day under its regular section 'Casualties and Offences', alongside reportage of another Yarra suicide discovery. The eighties were years of unprecedented prosperity and expansion for Melbourne, but life in the colonies was still too hard for many.

An inquest was held into the death of Jane Caldwell the day after she was found. Early Bird Hotel was the court. Twelve men were summonsed from the community – 'good and lawful men of Collingwood' – to act as jurors. The body was laid out. Witness statements were read aloud; Rev. Caldwell's was clinical, perhaps because police had transcribed it.

'I have seen the body of the deceased shown to the jury. I identify it as that of Jane Caldwell my wife,' he said. 'She was 39 years of age. I brought her to Melbourne for medical advice. I have not the slightest suspicion that she has been met with foul play. I have no reason to suppose, indeed I feel certain, that neither Mr nor Mrs McEachran knew that she had any tendency to self-destruction. Deceased had been a Lunatic Asylum [sic] 9 or 10 years ago.'

Though no records of her earlier incarceration can be found, there is no reason to disbelieve Jane had been suffering her mental illness for a decade or more.

The finding of the 'Proceedings of inquest held upon the body of Jane Caldwell, of Collingwood, received at the Crown Law Office, April 19, 1883' was without a twist.

> The jury found that Jane Caldwell came by her death on the 17th April 1883, in the river Yarra at Collingwood. She was found drowned. There is no evidence to show how she became

drowned but the jury are of the mind that she drowned herself whilst labouring under temporary insanity.

Rev. Caldwell did not stay single for long. Two-and-a-half years later he was engaged to another wealthy Tasmanian. Her name was Marian Whitesides, eldest daughter of James Whitesides, a successful furniture maker and owner of a well-known shop in Hobart. The Whitesides family was connected to Jane Caldwell's family (the Lindsays) by marriage. In short, one of Jane's nieces had married Marian's younger brother. Rev. James Caldwell married Marian Whitesides in October 1885. Another Presbyterian minister – Rev. James Beattie, of Launceston – performed the ceremony.

It was never recorded in any family documents how the eight Caldwell children found out their mother was dead. The 'little ones' were too young to understand. School-aged Hugh, Willie and Jim were old enough to mourn and elder siblings Alice and Tom suffered even more from their loss. Such was the shame brought by suicide in those days, the tragic death of Jane Caldwell was never mentioned to anyone outside the family. However, her children, who had inherited their mumma's compassion and kindness, talked to each other about their earliest memories during times of joy, despair, boredom, confusion, frustration and excitement of that ascending decade.

One special moment together would be the 1887 Queen's Jubilee celebration – the fiftieth anniversary of the coronation of Queen Victoria – in Melbourne. Like thousands of others, the older Caldwells – Tom, Alice, Jim, Willie and Hugh – went to the city to see millions of lanterns hung outside houses and buildings in celebration of Her Majesty. The press said it was 'like a dream of Fairyland'. Alice would always remember how wonderful it was 'trotting around' with her brothers, 'looking at the illuminations'.

By then 'Marvellous Melbourne' was one of the largest cities in the world. The Caldwell children were also coming of age. Alice wanted the boys to stay close to home but they all had different ambitions. Tom was eyeing off land in Tasmania. Jim had taken an office job. Willie was headed to medical school. Only Hugh was intent on staying at The Point, where he could keep hunting and fishing with his best mate, Charlie Allchin. And in the winter he could play his favourite game.

II

Sons of Brightest Promise

Nine

Thirty years after the rules of an indigenous football code were drawn up in a public hotel, the sport had become a permanent mutation in Melbourne's marrow. A big league – the Victorian Football Association – was attracting thousands of spectators to each city match. Players were being praised in the press for being 'stout-hearted, quick-limbed young fellows who dare do all that becomes a man'. And country towns were organising committees to make teams that would compete against each other. No longer the gentlemen's winter hobby, 'Australian rules' was for everyone. In 1887 it was Mornington's turn to take the field.

Old newspapers provide the earliest record of football matches in Mornington. The *South Bourke and Mornington Journal* printed weekly news for readers living in Melbourne's south, east and Mornington Peninsula until the late 1880s. The broadsheet was only four pages but always had a column for sporting results and previews. From autumn to spring this was 'Football'.

In 1889, the *Mornington Standard* became the paper of record for the region. Each edition covered matches comprehensively and sometimes ran columns to promote the code. Like this one:

> The game becomes harder and more severe every year. Let our country teams show by their skill in the battle field and their amiability in the piping times of peace, that the estimation in which football is held shall increase and not diminish and show that the highly popular game of leather hoisting develops all the robust virile qualities which distinguish the true man from the simpering, knock-kneed, bullet headed dude.

The *Standard* did not employ sportswriters, instead relying on contributions from club members. The correspondent for the first team in the district, Frankston, was an unnamed player or players with an eye for news – often writing about controversy or conflict, which, in turn, created even more interest in the games. In such media copy, rivalries are born and nurtured.

Mornington's first football match was due to be played against Frankston on 11 June 1887, but a mistake 'in consequence of an error on the part of the [Mornington] club secretary' meant it had to be rescheduled.

The *South Bourke and Mornington Journal* reported on Wednesday 15 June 1887 that the game was now set for the following Saturday afternoon, adding, 'A close and exciting game is expected, and it is creating quite a stir amongst the young men of Mornington.'

It's likely the stir came from longstanding impatience.

Football had been invented in 1858. Since then, teams had been in Melbourne, then Geelong, and throughout the gold-rush towns.

Belatedly, it was the Mornington Peninsula's turn to join the playing ranks. No league had been established and Mornington had not even formed a committee by 1887. The leading residents were cobbling together a side to test the appetite for the game among players and barrackers.

The first game between Mornington and Frankston went ahead on a gentleman landowner's cleared paddock. Spectators in long coats and warm socks outlined the oval. The match report, published four days later in the *Journal*, wasn't exhaustive.

> After some very tough play the match resulted in a victory for the latter [Frankston] by 4 goals to nil.

'Tough play' was code for a game heavy on violence and light on skill, full of rugby-style scrimmaging, the code's worst feature.

Since Wills and the others had listed the first rules, administrators of clubs and the few leagues that existed had tweaked football laws to move away from what rugby watchers would call a 'rolling maul'. A breakthrough had been delivered by Henry Colden Antwill Harrison, a relation of Wills and one of the first Australian rules champions. During his playing days, Harrison was called 'the fastest man in football'; he pioneered running and bouncing at the same time and educated other players about the skill of punting to a target. Another development was called a 'little mark'.

Little marks (or catching) from short kicks were difficult to defend. Such strategic passages began giving spectators pleasure equal to seeing brutal collisions. A mixture of both these attractions within one game gave footballers and barrackers excitement they had never known.

Throughout the 1860s and '70s, the new game's character continued to mature, with an offside law being abolished, and players given freedom to roam after the kick-off. This was critical. The roaming is unique and sets it apart from other codes. Go anywhere. Do anything. Tom Wills was important here, too. In 1860 he had ordered his Richmond team to run ahead of the ball against Melbourne, taking advantage of the 'no offside'. James Coventry wrote in *Time and Space*, a history of the tactics of Australian rules: 'It is arguably the most important and influential tactical manoeuvre in the history of Australian football.'

Such advances passed quickly to the bush and teams tried to play the way they did in the city. But it would take time. A new generation would have to be born and raised on the game for it to be enlivened by impressive passing and forward play.

At least by the late 1880s the country teams had settled on the framework of uniforms (knickerbockers, jerseys and boots), number of players per team (twenty), shape of the ground (oval) and ball (same).

Two things can be taken from the report of that first Frankston-Mornington match. Four goals to nothing might not sound a big margin but in those days it was a shellacking. Frankston obviously had players with some experience in running and little marks. More significantly, the win gifted a month of grandstanding rights to the victors. Frankston would prove itself to be a world-class boaster. Mornington people copped defeat well in that first season. No big deal. Players shared in toasts and songs at the after-match social. But in the coming years the losses would mount and the boys from The Point would soon despise being outscored.

In 1888, Mornington decided to officially form a football club. The first challenge for the administrators was to find a ground to play on. Mornington Park, where cricket, summer picnics and all other outdoor social events were staged, was not an option. Heavy boots would churn the turf into mud and maybe leave the open space disfigured for the holiday season. A field had to be found away from the shoreline. This turned out to be no problem at all. Farmers offered their cleared paddocks. One without tree stumps and manure was preferred.

The club's number-one benefactor was George Stooke, who lived in a small house called 'Wolfdene', originally built in 1858 as the Mornington Hotel upon a 26-acre property. Stooke had previously owned a successful butcher shop in Flinders Street, Melbourne, and had also travelled widely. He no longer worked – his official title on shire documents was 'gentleman' – but was active in community life.

Any new club had to find a way of raising money for balls, posts and equipment. This would be easy. By 1888, Mornington was a very sociable town; fundraisers for the school and other groups were held each weekend in Main Street at the Mechanics' Institute, a handsome brick building used as a community hall and library. The team would be able to pull a crowd for a drink and dance after matches. Also, it was decided to appeal for members to sign up and pay dues, so money could be raised before the season. The Mornington Football Club formation meeting was scheduled for mid-April. The *South Bourke and Mornington Journal* made the announcement:

> A football club of over 80 members has recently been formed at the Point, and through the kindness of Mr. G. F. Stooke secured a suitable piece of ground for playing upon, part of that gentleman's property.

Richard Waycott, a leading businessman, was elected club secretary and captain. He was a smart choice. A top all-round sportsman, his leadership was critical for stability in those teething seasons, as other players tried to understand the game's rules and patterns. He started being quoted in the press:

> Mr Waycott, the secretary and captain, informs me that the team about to play a series of matches, though at present raw, have some good stuff in them, and are likely to give a creditable account of themselves during the season.

Away from the field, Waycott was planning to take on management of the soon-to-be-built Coffee Palace. He was now involved in the two most exciting developments in Mornington.

In early May, and twice more during the year, the new Mornington football team played against the powerful Frankston club. Waycott trained his men every week on Thursday after work. Those who could attend puffed and sweated in the brief twilight, kicking, passing, talking, smoking pipes and laughing.

With full effort, football practice can be almost as fun as playing. The movement of the ball among players feels more elegant than it is; leg muscles bulge as boots turn and push off the soft grass; steam rises from shoulders and heads like tiny stacks of chimney smoke. The exercise and fellowship gives a sense of euphoria, or at least an escape from the drudgery of work or household chores. And it comes with the promise of competition. All of a sudden, Saturday seems so close.

Also training for the upcoming matches was Frankston, under the watch of captain Jack Sadleir, the most revered sportsman in the district, a star cricketer who made centuries for his town while others fancied twenty a top score, and an ace on the football field, having played for Essendon in the Melbourne competition in 1886 and 1887.

Sadleir would probably have stood out even without his athletic prowess. He was the son of John Sadleir, the Police Superintendent in charge of country town Glenrowan when notorious bushranger Ned Kelly was captured after a shoot-out.

Jack Sadleir had resisted following his father into the police service. Instead, he managed a bank. For the next four years he would be both captain and secretary of Frankston, admired as a match winner and cursed by Mornington players, though not necessarily disliked.

In 1888, Sadleir's limbs were light and strong and his motivation high. He led his team onto Stooke's paddock on the second wet Saturday in May. An anonymous Frankston player (probably Sadleir) wrote the match report for the following Wednesday's edition of the *South Bourke and Mornington Journal*.

The reporter generously acknowledged that the 'newly formed club has a large number of subscribers and some promising players, who, under the training of their energetic secretary and captain, Mr. Waycott, should become a good team'. As for the match itself, it seemed likely to be postponed due to rain, but got underway at about 3 pm.

Despite playing 'several men short', Frankston kicked the game's opening goal, which was 'greatly cheered'. However, Mornington fought back and kicked a goal. The locals scored again minutes later but it was 'disputed by the Frankston players' and disallowed by the umpire.

The undermanned visiting team then kicked its second goal. 'The play then went on until the ball and players could scarcely be distinguished from one end of the ground to the other, until time was called and the play ceased.' The final result was a matter of opinion, 'the Frankston team claiming two goals to one and the Mornington claiming a draw'.

'However, under all circumstances,' the *South Bourke and Mornington Journal* concluded, 'the Frankston players, who proved so successful last season, found on this occasion a team, though young, worthy of their steel. The usual courtesies were accorded to the visiting team by the Mornington team. The next match between these clubs will be played on the Frankston ground.'

Both teams were pleased. Mornington looked the part and could claim a draw. And the Frankston men could smile at the win, as they saw it. It was the closest match between the two teams for the season. They would play again two months later, Frankston winning without doubt. Reports varied in length, with less interesting contests receiving only a few paragraphs. The *South Bourke and Mornington Journal* published the following brief from Mornington v Frankston II, 1888:

> The anticipated close contest did not come off, the Frankston players proving too good for the Mornington, scoring three goals and sundry behinds to sundry behinds on the part of Mornington.

Despite the score, football became a favourite pastime in Mornington within that first season. The few other daytime winter entertainments suffered by comparison. These included the Mornington Farmers' Society Annual Ploughing Match. Suddenly ploughmen trudging through quagmires, often sinking into the bog, and a few horses jumping for a modest prize, didn't thrill as it once might have. No, from now on the game of Australian rules would be *the* Saturday afternoon habit for players, families and friends. Frankston played fourteen games in 1888 and Mornington played a similar number. Mornington's match reports weren't as consistently printed in the local newspaper so it is impossible to know every result.

It was a bleak winter, wetter than usual. The rain coming across the bay seemed never to break. Queen's Birthday weekend, usually one of the biggest on the local businesses' calendar, was all but drowned by a deluge. Steamers from Melbourne were absent or empty, though some people did make it to The Point: a team of footballers from Brighton.

The game was played in a wind too strong for headwear, as the *Caulfield and Elsternwick Leader* reported:

> BRIGHTON v MORNINGTON:
> The Brighton journeyed on Queen's birthday to Mornington to play the local team. The play started at 3 o'clock, during which time it rained very hard at intervals and a strong wind blew across the ground. The game was very evenly contested, and resulted in a win for the Brighton by 1 goal and 7 behinds to 9 behinds.

A Mornington correspondent wrote a separate report for the *Mornington Journal*:

> The Mornington were captained by Waycott, who says he will find a way to make the, as yet raw, Mornington team equal, if not superior, to any in the country – so Frankston and Dandenong clubs may look out for their laurels.

The freezing crowd from the Brighton match adjourned to the Mechanics' Institute to warm up and toast Her Majesty. The visitors stayed and joined in the singing and dancing. This event was old Schnapper Point's first fancy-dress ball. Dozens of couples dressed up, and a piano was played all night. The drinkers favoured rum. Smoke and dance overtook the room and the party lasted until five o'clock the next morning, outlasting the town's kerosene lamps by six hours or so. (The only other person up that late at night was the 'nightman', employed to empty 'nightsoil' from the town's outhouses.)

Next morning, church gossip was worth the price of the collection bowl. Parishioners with red eyes and stale liquor perfume might have been sheepish, if not still buzzing from a top night out.

Optimism around the new football team's chances of winning was a bit unrealistic. Mornington's season continued with a match against a city church team called St Peter's. Again, Mornington played host. It was becoming obvious other teams were happy to come to the bay's shore for their football fix. The St Peter's lads enjoyed their brief stay, kicking four goals to one for an easy win. Waycott's men then hosted two more teams in a week. Melbourne telegraph operators came for a Wednesday match and scored two goals to Mornington's one. Three days later North Park (from Hotham, near Melbourne) kicked two goals to nought.

In July, Mornington welcomed another team, the 'Wanderers', from Melbourne. These blokes knew what they were doing and dominated, scoring seven goals to one. The frowns of defeat lasted only a few minutes after the bell. Some of the Wanderers joined the locals for a concert and dance that lasted a long time and raised a few pounds for the committee. Again, tipsy stragglers were seen outside the unfinished façade of the Mechanics' Institute in the dark morning hours, slapping backs, swaying and sucking in the frigid past-midnight air.

Other fundraisers were held. In August, the football club held an athletics carnival. The short season was nearly done. In September, 'the Mornington', as it was called, had some success, securing apparently its second win for the season, although the first was not recorded.

The *South Bourke and Mornington Journal* reported the contest against St Kilda, not yet a member of football's highest-ranking league:

> After some exciting and capital play on both sides resulted in a win for Mornington by three goals and thirteen behinds to one goal and three behinds. The Mornington team have been very unsuccessful this season, this being only the second match they have won during the season.

The match was blighted by umpire abuse and a punch-up.

> During the game one of the visitors made use of some very unbecoming language to the umpire, H. Worrell, which resulted in blows being struck. The more sensible members of both teams interfered (sic) what might have been an unseemly row.

The Mornington lads went to Sorrento by dray the next week. Sorrento had a surprisingly strong team, despite its relative isolation at the peninsula's southern tip, and won four goals to nil. The surface of the local field was a shock to the visitors. It turned out the sandy coast that Collins had found unsuitable for a lasting settlement was good for a home-team advantage.

> The Mornington players were, as a Cornishman would say, 'all abroad' when they had to tackle play on a ground composed of sand hills, and were no match for the Sorrento boys on their own ground – or on their own sand.

It had been a long succession of matches for the newcomers and after the city-based South Melbourne Football Club sent its second team to play in Mornington, inflicting upon the locals another defeat, the end of the 1888 season was welcome. A concert at the Mechanics' Institute was given to the players from both teams.

The warm weather was returning and so was cricket. Another sports carnival followed. Men and women competed against each other in events like the 150-yard sprint, cricket-ball throwing, pole vault (the record being eight feet), the 100-yard dash for runners over forty (each place-getter awarded prizes, including a driving whip and a book by Shakespeare), hurdles and football kicking.

A grand ball was held after this athletic event. This time, more than a hundred couples came to the party, some in fancy garb. Some of the dresses attracted comments for days, if not weeks. One lady came dressed as 'winter', in a black cashmere dress covered with 'silver snow flakes'.

On all available evidence, Mornington's earliest efforts in Australian rules were successful, if not triumphant. Wins and losses should never be the only measure of a team. The club had hosted almost every game, travelled occasionally and socialised every week. Members were smiling at the prospect of future football seasons.

Ten

The eldest Caldwell brother, Tom, was the first exceptional sportsman from Mornington to play football in Melbourne. In 1885 the tall, dark-haired boy attended Scotch College and held an esteemed place in the 'First Twenty', competing regularly against teams from Melbourne Grammar, Geelong Grammar and Wesley College. The Victorian schools competition was vigorous, fast and skilful; its standard was among the highest in the colonies.

Without doubt, Tom would have been Mornington's best player in the club's earliest seasons but he never played for his hometown. By the late 1880s he had graduated from Scotch and moved to Tasmania to build a house on land inherited from his grandfather William Lindsay. However, he once gave the boys from The Point some coaching. It proved to be an unlikely catalyst for the district's first major football controversy.

In autumn 1889 Tom heard that the Mornington team was training for its second full season of matches. On a short visit home, he called in to Stooke's property for a look. Tom was twenty-two years old, athletic and stronger than ever from clearing trees in the Tasmanian bush. He was also naturally competitive from all those years spent racing his siblings around the broad, green gardens of his childhood.

When he was about ten, Tom entered his first sporting contest. The local workmen were hosting a carnival, with running races, throwing contests, and a tug of war. Tom convinced his father to let him go to Mornington Park. Jane Caldwell would not let one of her children go out in public without impeccable dress and she made no exception this day, making sure Tom wore a brand new straw hat.

Later in the day, Rev. Caldwell wandered down to the foreshore to watch the fun. He saw a race being prepared. The local councillor and baths owner, William Irvine, sidled up to the minister.

'The fellow in the old hat will win,' Irvine said.

The fellow was Tom, who proceeded to outrun the men and claim first prize. Rev. Caldwell didn't know until it was over that the winner was his son, whose straw hat was already dirty and falling apart. Tom was smiling when he came home, but the household considered his victory a mixed result. His mother, at least, was upset by people calling her eldest a 'ragamuffin' and the 'most untidy boy in the park'.

The ragamuffin had now grown into a would-be gentleman of strong opinions. Tom watched the Mornington football team kicking to each other in the dimming light on a Thursday evening and declared the practice a shambles. He told Waycott and the other players he thought they did not know what they were doing.

'I tell you what, you fellows,' he said, 'you don't play football at all. You don't know or keep to rules, or anything else. That may be shinty you play, but it is certainly not football.'

The local boys were probably bemused by his reference to shinty, a game played in Scotland and Ireland. It was a strange comparison to make, considering Tom Caldwell had never seen shinty. He was born in Ireland but did not know the country at all.

Still, Tom continued with his criticisms, perhaps too cocksure to notice he might be resented. 'I will give you some lessons while I am home, if you like, and you ought to make a good team, for there's plenty of bone and muscle among you.'

His coaching tips can only be guessed. But since all football followers desired a faster and more skilful game, it can be assumed he educated the team in passing the ball, perhaps stressing the 'little mark' as a means of keeping the ball away from the opposition while moving within scoring range. To reinforce his teachings, Tom arranged an Easter holiday scratch match between Mornington Football Club and a team of 'School Boys'. There is no record of the participants but it is certain Tom led a side of educated and wealthy sons of peninsula landowners, featuring the Caldwells (Jim had played football at school and Willie was currently boarding at Scotch) and some of their classmates, as well as visiting pupils from Geelong and Melbourne grammars. It is likely Charlie Allchin played; he was now boarding at Wesley in Melbourne but came home regularly. Hugh Caldwell was still at Mornington State School in 1889. But he might have played, considering he was always the strongest boy of his age.

The Mornington team, described as a 'heavy one', was made from local tradesmen, labourers and fishermen. It took courage for the students to go up against such men, though the School Boys were hardly a bunch of weak city dwellers. If they were holidaying in Mornington they were fit and durable from hunting, swimming and fishing.

Tom Caldwell was the stand-out performer in the scratch match and the School Boys won. The game gave everyone a much-needed workout for the coming winter but at what cost? Throughout the 1889 and 1890 seasons there was creeping disharmony within the Mornington club. Some players began to complain about the town's richer members having 'too much to say'.

A letter from local schoolteacher and businessman Joseph Worrell to a friend (Charlie Allchin's older brother, Tom, who was living in Queensland at the time), best explains the rift:

> The football club was a very mixed affair, and certain of the members came to think that the 'toffs' (as they call them) ran the club so they split and formed a separate club called the Rovers; this opposition club has attracted to it, all the larrikin element, and consequently the senior club has been mainly composed of all the better class of fellows in the place.

The argument was not one-sided. The 'toffs' claimed there were some teammates who drank too much after matches and had 'brought disgrace on the whole place'. Much of the antipathy was bloated by egos. In reality, there was no clear divide between classes. Most of the team was hard working, whether they were employers or employees. Anyway, attempts to make peace failed at the start of the 1891 season, when this curious article appeared in the *Mornington Standard*:

> The Mornington Football Club has this season been thoroughly re-constructed. Mr J. Wall has been appointed secretary and is assiduously pushing the interests of the club in all directions. A strong and popular committee has been appointed, who are doing their best to forward the interests of the club.

The same newspaper edition ran another story by a different, unnamed writer, one of the so-called toffs:

> A second football club has been started at Mornington, called the Rovers, composed of the discontented members principally of the old club. The subscription has been fixed at 2s 6d per member, consequently it is being patronised by lads of the wide rimmed hat and bell bottomed trouser following.

Men who toiled in the sun for their living wore the widest hats in the town and on the bay. This commentary on dress standards was particularly scathing and hurtful. If there had been any hope of a truce between the warring Mornington factions, it was damaged by this barely disguised contempt. There were arguments in Main Street over who had written the piece. A week of bitterness and hostility forced the Mornington club secretary, telegraph operator James Wall, to write an apologetic letter to the *Standard* editor, for urgent publishing:

> Sir, - A paragraph appeared in your last issue, about the rival teams in Mornington, and characterises the Rovers club as an offshoot of the Mornington Football Club, and that their ranks are composed of (to use a vulgar term) the followers of the broad brimmed hats and bell bottomed fraternity. Consequently on this paragraph appearing, I and my committee are blamed as the writers of same. I am now instructed to write you, that my committee repudiate the authorship, and to express their regret that the article in question should have appeared, as it tends to open up a wide breach and cause a deal of friction, both individually on and off the football field.

Wall's note did not prevent the Rovers forging ahead and fielding a side in the 1891 district competition. Differences could now be settled on the oval. A match was soon scheduled between the original Mornington team and its newest rival.

Eleven

Hugh Caldwell, youngest player on the field, had taken the mark before the cowbell rang. His kick would now determine whether his teammates drew with the Rovers or whether his side would suffer the embarrassment of being beaten by the debutants.

He squared his body with the goals and prepared to take a few steps before kicking. The Rovers players and barrackers wanted so badly to win they could barely watch Hugh take his shot.

There is no newspaper record of what happened next. The recollection of Hugh's after-the-siren attempt came from his sister, Alice Caldwell, who was watching nervously. Alice would later write a short book about her family. She called it *Love's Tribute*. Among other prose, it contains one of the first – if not best – pieces of Australian country football writing.

Of the earlier stages, she wrote:

Mornington was built to resemble splendid English seaside villages, but at its heart was a working harbour. Baskets of fish were hauled in boats to the city, and timber (neatly stacked in this early 1880s picture) was sold as railway sleepers or firewood. *Courtesy: Mornington and District Historical Society*

This photo of Main Street was taken in the early 1890s from the roof of the Coffee Palace. General stores, banks, workshops and stables provided for the working class and wealthy holiday-house owners. *Courtesy: Mornington and District Historical Society*

English couple Sarah Jagger and Thomas Allchin were married in Melbourne on 2 June 1857. This is their wedding photo. By the 1890s they were esteemed leaders of the community, with a son in the local football team.
Courtesy: Janet Groves

After finishing his schooling in Mornington, Charlie Allchin boarded at Wesley College in Melbourne and became a trainee architect. On weekends he liked to return to Mornington to visit his family, play football and spend time with his best friend, Hugh Caldwell.
Courtesy: Janet Groves

Sarah Allchin managed the best general store in Mornington. She once wrote in her diary, 'I am sure for 18 years I worked 18 hours a day.' *Courtesy: Mornington and District Historical Society*

The Allchins lived in a mansion called Sutton Grange. They built it with a tower overlooking the harbour. Sarah Allchin stood on this tower to watch the search for her son Charlie and the other lost footballers on the Queen's Birthday weekend in 1892. *Courtesy: Mornington and District Historical Society*

Born and educated in Northern Ireland, Rev. James Caldwell came to Australia with his first wife, who died soon after. He became the 'exceedingly popular' and 'genial' Presbyterian minister of Melbourne inner-suburb Collingwood and gold-mining town Maryborough before settling in Mornington in 1874. *Courtesy: Janette Allen*

A 'naturally delicate woman', Jane Caldwell (nee Lindsay) had nine children with Rev. Caldwell. Jane suffered depression and committed suicide by drowning in the Yarra River in 1883. She was thirty-nine. *Courtesy: Janette Allen*

Tom Caldwell (left) was the eldest child. Jim is on the right. Note the fancy clothes. The family was always wealthy, due to Jane Caldwell's inheritance. When the town split into two classes over a football controversy, the Caldwells were described as 'toffs'.
Courtesy: Janette Allen

Jim Caldwell was living in Tasmania in 1892, but came to visit his family for the Queen's Birthday weekend, deciding to play football at the last minute. It would be the first time Jim, Willie and Hugh Caldwell would play a game in the same side.
Courtesy: Janette Allen

Apprentice carpenter Hugh Caldwell was the outstanding young footballer in the district. By the time he was seventeen he was a leading goal scorer for the Mornington club. He once kicked a goal 'that had it been done on the MCG they would've carried him off the field shoulders high'. *Courtesy: Janette Allen*

Alice Caldwell was the second eldest sibling. She was like a second mother to her brothers. Seen here as a young girl, she would grow into the family's chief storyteller. In her book *Love's Tribute*, she provided one of the best passages of colonial-era country football ever written. *Courtesy: Janette Allen*

Willie Caldwell grew from a sickly child into an admired cadet soldier and medical student. Curiously, whenever he played football for Mornington he attracted the ire of opposition barrackers. *Courtesy: Janette Allen*

Willie Caldwell (bottom right) was a popular boarder at Scotch College in Melbourne. In 1890 he was a senior member of the cadet corps that won the prestigious Lady Loch colours for performing militarily better than any in the colony. *Courtesy: Scotch College archives*

The three youngest Caldwell children were Jack, Sallie and Jeannie. Their parents and older siblings called them 'the little ones'. Here they are with the family dog in the mid-1880s. *Courtesy: Janette Allen*

Process captain Charles Hooper was a footballer, fisherman and regatta sailor. On the Thursday before the Queen's Birthday weekend in 1892, he proposed to sail his teammates to the next match. Previously, Mornington had only ever travelled to away games by railway or horse-drawn carriage. *Courtesy: Mornington and District Historical Society*

This mysterious photograph (date unknown) is said to be the only picture of the *Process*. *Courtesy: Mornington and District Historical Society*

A picture taken from a couta boat at the spot the *Process* was foundering when located by searchers in 1892. See how close it is to the shore – and note the rocky reef leading to the cliffs. *Courtesy: Paul Kennedy*

Nearing midnight, news passed around the town that the footballers had not come home. Over at the Caldwell mansion, Rev. Caldwell could not sleep. Eventually he went to see the policeman, Senior Constable Murphy. The minister said in a broken voice, 'My three sons are with the party.' *Courtesy: Janette Allen*

After the tragedy, the *Australasian* newspaper hired an artist to illustrate its coverage. Here, pairs and small groups of people awaited news from the search boats. The small lighthouse was one of two lights guiding the footballers home. Another light was fixed to the pier. Gas lighting had recently been introduced to Mornington.

Two men on the pier pointing to the sad sight of the *Wanderer* – flag lowered – towing the *Process* back to the harbour. The other fishing boats are in the background.

This sketch shows the broken *Process* after the accident. The boat would later be repaired and sailed by the late Charles Hooper's fisherman son George.

The most shocking of all the sketches depicts locals carrying the corpse of Alfred Lawrence into the mail cart. Lawrence's father was no longer standing by. He had told Senior Constable Thomas Murphy to arrange carriage of his son to the family's general store.

1. THE WANDERER SIGHTING THE SUBMERGED BOAT PROCESS ON THE MORNING OF SUNDAY, THE 22ND INST. 2. RAISING OF THE BOAT PROCESS BY THE CREW OF THE WANDERER. (FROM SKETCHES SUPPLIED BY YACHTSMEN ON BOARD THE WANDERER.)
PORTRAITS OF THOSE WHO WERE LOST IN THE BOAT PROCESS. (FROM PHOTOGRAPHS.)

THE MORNINGTON CATASTROPHE.

The player portraits were penned from photographs provided to the *Leader* newspaper by families. The wrecked boat picture – with naked Alfred Lawrence lying across the thwart – was sketched from accounts given by *Wanderer* crewmen. The small insert shows the *Wanderer* sailing toward the *Process*.

On Sunday, while fishermen searched the bay for the missing team, Rev. Caldwell attempted to hold his weekly sermon. Melbourne newspaper *The Argus* reported, 'The officiating minister broke down in the middle of his prayers and was compelled to beg the indulgence of the congregation.'

Arthur Peck (seen here in his nineties) was the sailor who led the recovery of the *Process* on the Sunday morning. He had been staying the weekend with his friend H. P. Fergie on the famed yacht *Wanderer* in Mornington harbour. *Courtesy: Peck family*

Tom Caldwell never stopped grieving for his three brothers. Years after the accident he left his property in Tasmania and moved to Western Australia looking for gold. He later settled in Gippsland, Victoria, marrying Jessie Craig. *Courtesy: Janette Allen*

Rev. Caldwell served the Mornington community for a record twenty-eight years. He installed a plaque in his church to remember his sons, with the message, 'They were lovely and pleasant in their lives and in their death they were not divided.' The plaque is still there.

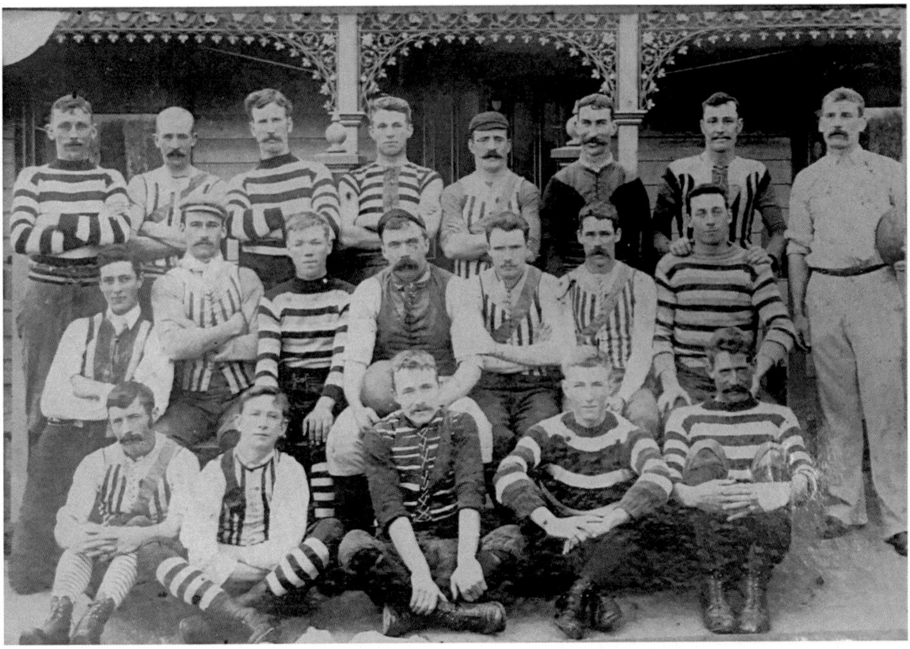

This team photo is the earliest of Mornington Football Club, probably from the 1895 season. Tom Coxhell, captain of the 1892 side, is in the middle, second from the right. He is wearing a sash, which is probably blue. It was not unusual for country teams to have different striped jerseys, as each player had to buy his own.

The baker Tom Coxhell as an old man. After having a 'presentiment' of doom and balking at riding home in Hooper's *Process*, Coxhell lived another sixty-eight years.

An early photograph of the memorial erected in 1893 on the corner of Main Street and The Esplanade. Until recently, most thought it a remembrance of war. But the Mornington and District Historical Society complemented it with an information board in 2012 and now more strollers stop to read about the 'Fifteen Young Men'.

> Mornington, which represented the old original club of the place felt they had not only their own honour to uphold, but felt that of all former members, for the 'Rovers,' compared with themselves, were comparatively a new club, and they were therefore determined to save themselves from being 'done' by the Rovers, as Hughie put it. The Rovers, on the other hand, with victory almost in sight, were equally ready to fight for it with unabating energy.

Alice lathered Hugh with soapy praise. But her brother's stature was not too embellished. Though he was only sixteen, he was one of the team's best, a sportsman of rare promise.

Hugh had not followed his brothers into high education. Instead, he was an apprentice carpenter. On leaving the local state school with his certificate, Hugh had to decide whether he wanted to go to Scotch College like his brothers or go to work. He had approached his father and said he wanted to be a land developer. Rev. Caldwell told him he needed to 'go into a profession'.

'You can be a carpenter,' his father said. With the skills of a builder, Hugh could later branch out.

The timing was perfect. The colony's property boom had lasted the entire 1880s. When Hugh started swinging a hammer, development in Mornington was at its peak. Rev. Caldwell approached the busiest builder in town to take on his son as an apprentice. His name was Joseph Dale (J. D.) Grover, son of William Grover, one of Thomas Allchin's contemporaries. J. D. Grover would prove to be a wonderful mentor to Hugh. As well as being a hard worker, Grover was one of the best sportsmen in the district. He seemed to be an older, horseshoe-moustached version of Hugh Caldwell.

Away from work, Hugh was a hunter and fisherman. His body was tanned and responded well to long days in the sun's glare, unlike those men born in Britain. Sometimes his fellow workers complained about the summer heat, insisting it was fit only for a 'black man'. Hugh didn't know what they were grumbling about. He was an Australian child, who knew no different.

In the past he had won many matches of cricket and football for the pupils and staff at Mornington State School. His upgrade to senior football was not difficult, and he was given the position of 'forward', the old version of a 'full forward', always roaming near the opposition's 'fortress' or 'citadel', as it was often called in those days.

The younger children of the town adored Hugh so much they had taken to following him from end to end, moving as a flock during the quarter-time, half-time and three-quarter-time rests. The children saw Hugh as their representative. As Alice Caldwell noted, it was not long ago that Hugh had been 'one of them', sorting out their schoolyard fights, giving no mercy to bullies, organising games in the playground.

Before each senior match, children used to ask Hugh if they could mind his hat while he played. His boyish face smiled and he handed over his cap. Now the adults were shepherding the children away from Hugh so he could concentrate. The talented youngster preferred a punt to a place kick. Other players in that era chose to kick the ball balanced on a mound of dirt or held at the tip by a teammate. Some favoured a drop kick. Hugh, however, trusted his skill to drop the ball carefully to his boot, without it wobbling on the way down. He now prepared to send 'the ball off on its perilous and decisive journey', as Alice wrote.

'Stand back, you fellows,' Hughie apparently called out to those invading his periphery. 'Stand back.'

Barrackers and Rovers kept encroaching. Hugh's teammates stood guard.

'He was certainly within a very difficult angle of the goal posts,' Alice wrote. 'There he stood, calm and still, while Morningtonites and Rovers surged round him, the Rovers ready to spring and catch the ball as it rose in the air; the Mornington men struggling to hold them back, so that it might go on its course unimpeded.'

'Stand back,' Hugh said a third time.

The umpire, Senior Constable Murphy, echoed the instruction. This helped calm the crowd. Tom Caldwell was there – on another visit from Tasmania – dressed in three layers of clothing, including a long coat, urging everyone back a little. He had wanted to play the game but the Rovers protested against it, pointing out he was no longer a resident. (Jim and Willie had not come home from Melbourne for the weekend and did not play or watch this game.)

Eventually the players from both sides stopped shoving and watched Hugh drop the ball onto his boot's laces.

Alice Caldwell noted:

> He was outwardly calm and cool, while they were all visibly excited. Inwardly, he was excited himself, for I, standing at the seeable distance, could see that his ruddy cheek grew pale, and that a set determined look gathered round his mouth, but

> he had the magnificent nerve of our father, and when the right moment came, the ball was sent flying into the air far above the Rovers standing by, who made one frantic spring to catch it, and then, with a cry of dismay, watched it as it soared above the goal posts, turning in mid-air, and falling between them, amid breathless silence.

Hats and cheers rent the air. The Rovers felt robbed but only for a few minutes. A draw is usually an empty result but sometimes it can be fair. And in Mornington, during that period of class-driven angst, it must have been a relief to all but those with the heaviest chips on their shoulders.

Alice recounted that the Caldwells did not all go straight home after the match. It was her Saturday-evening ritual to visit an elderly friend. It was dark when she finally arrived back at the manse. The whole house smelled of the eucalyptus oil Hugh had worn during the game. She found him in his room.

'May I come in?' she asked.

Her brother was getting dressed. 'Hold on,' he said, before calling out that he was ready for her visit.

'You are a darling,' she said. 'You kicked the goal magnificently.'

He shrugged and said, 'I would have been a fool to have missed it.'

'Well, most men would have under similar circumstances,' said Alice.

Rev. Caldwell was in the drawing room, preparing his Sunday sermon before a healthy log fire. He had not watched football that day or any other. He would have preferred his sons were kicking around topics for a debating team. Hugh, Alice, Tom and the little ones – Jeannie, Jack and Sallie – had gathered in the breakfast room for tea when their father entered and said, 'Well, Hugh, how about the football this afternoon?'

'My word,' Tom said to his papa. 'Hughie kicked a goal today that had it been done on the MCG, they would've carried him off the field shoulders high.'

'Ah' was all Rev. Caldwell said.

Twelve

Charlie Allchin hurried soft-footed along the wide city footpaths, sliding past and through and around the other people. He was determined not to touch anyone or anything. The 'disease-haunted' Melbourne had courted sickness every year since the rush for gold had waned and the children of miners had moved back into the capital. But 1891 had been worse than the others. A silent killer called influenza was moving among the population, felling victims at a fearful rate. As he walked along the banks of the bloated Yarra River, closing in on the Melbourne Terminus, Charlie kept his lips pressed and hands in his pockets. He had a bag slung over one shoulder. He was heading home.

Melbourne residents had lived through two floods in a year. Relief funds were still being raised for people left homeless by the June disaster. At the time it was a 'great' flood. But then more rain fell in the mountains to the east, and within a day the Yarra burst again and the city folk were wading through the 'greatest flood on record'.

Lower reaches of Collingwood and other bank-side suburbs went under. The river widened to 'prodigious proportions' and submerged parts of the city centre. Homes, shops, factories and suburban railways were all damaged. Much of the colony saw flash flooding, the type that doesn't need a river or creek to cause mayhem. This all came with news the Depression was deepening. The boom was now officially over.

'Marvellous Melbourne' – the empire's brightest new toy – was busted. Banks were closing weekly, people were killing themselves, whole suburbs were empty and the homeless slept where they could. When the rain stopped and impromptu inland lakes quit rising, gangs of men were at least employed to go and fix everything; the train lines came first, so the people didn't have to sit in one spot being miserable, they could at least move around feeling glum.

Charlie had been stranded in the city until the railway to the peninsula was declared safe. He was relieved to hear he could return home to see his parents. Unusually, Mornington had caught Melbourne's flu. Much of the townsfolk were apparently bedridden. He wanted to go and help. After buying his ticket, he found a seat on the next 'iron horse' south.

Sarah and Thomas Allchin's youngest child, Charlie, was now a nineteen-year-old graduate of Wesley College. He was living in South Yarra, across the river from the city, and working – doing his 'articles' – for a leading architect. Without really planning it he had arrived on the doorstep of an elite industry shaping Melbourne's future. But he was no social climber – he was a country lad. And he always looked forward to going back to The Point. When the train started chugging, he exhaled and enjoyed feeling the power and acceleration beneath him.

Charlie had been a competent student at Mornington State School in the late 1870s and early 1880s. His earliest friend was Willie Caldwell. For years they complemented each other, even in looks. Willie's head was oval-shaped, his wide features occupying almost every inch of it. Charlie's face was long and fine, a bit like his thin-shouldered physique, though he was strong and fit from his bush upbringing. Charlie's hair colour had always been a riddle to be solved. It appeared to change in varying light. Mostly it was foxy red-brown. Sometimes it darkened. In summer, it looked blond.

If he were a child today the concerned adults in his life might label Charlie introverted. Back then his parents just noticed he was watchful. As he became more comfortable with others he revealed his wit. Mostly, he was happy in the company of large groups, where he could remain silent until he felt like delivering a well-timed sarcastic quip.

Willie was also a sarcastic boy.

He was the smartest kid in his class and was musically unmatched. In his final years at state school he helped his teachers organise concerts to raise money for the town's Mechanics' Institute (Rev. Caldwell was the chairman of the fundraising committee and Thomas Allchin the treasurer).

Willie wrote the programmes in his best handwriting. Charlie helped him. They performed in the concerts and were praised in the *Standard* for reciting 'polkas and gallops' they had memorised. 'A first class programme was provided, each piece being well rendered and in many cases vociferously applauded.'

Charlie and Willie's differences became more apparent as they approached adolescence. Charlie was not a vain kid and wore the practical clothes, anything with shorts. He often liked to say he 'preferred the ease of flannel'. Willie, on the other hand, had begun wearing whatever could accommodate a silk handkerchief in his breast pocket, for a splash of colour. One of the few times he didn't bother dressing to impress was when he challenged his brothers to boxing matches. He had a quick temper and could be steered into a stoush without effort. To settle arguments, and just for fun, he fought Tom, Jim and Hugh with gloves in the garden. Charlie would sit and watch, perhaps acting as unofficial judge, as the brothers danced around pretending they knew what they were doing. Most times, Hugh was Willie's sporting foe. Hugh would punch his way on top and Willie would cry out, 'Look out, Hugh, what are you driving at? What are you up to?' Charlie needn't score their fights. They usually ended in abandonment.

The hours after school and on weekends were spent by Charlie, Willie and, increasingly, Hugh, playing outdoors. Saturday afternoons hosted some type of athletic pursuit. And Sunday was for worship. After a few years of the Allchin family attending Rev. Caldwell's church, a Wesleyan chapel was built about five kilometres from Mornington. At 9.30 am, Sarah and Thomas Allchin could be seen with their children riding a low carriage basket northeast, towed by a slow horse everyone knew as Turpin, deliverer of groceries from the general store on weekdays. Thomas Allchin liked his horses snail-paced but reliable. One morning, as they passed the Caldwell house, Willie came to the family's eastern porch and said to his siblings in the breakfast room, 'I back him [Turpin] to do three miles in an hour.'

'If they hurry,' one of the others laughed. The Caldwells did not understand anyone going slow. Their horse was the fastest in town, or so they claimed.

In the early 1880s a new Wesleyan church was built closer to Main Street. Charlie was as thankful as Turpin they no longer had to go so far for their sermons. From then, he and the Caldwell brothers would all meet early Sunday mornings on the corner of Barkly Street and Tanti Avenue, just outside the manse, and walk into town together for their separate church services. When the preaching was done, they would meet up again. The Caldwells knew that if the Wesleyan minister was 'holding forth' – running overtime – Charlie was likely to be in a sour mood.

'He'll be in a scot,' Willie would say.

Jim and Willie would laugh when Charlie finally arrived. Only Hughie offered sympathy.

After church, Charlie liked to go to the Caldwells for a play until the dinner bell rang. Then young Allchin would head back to his house. Each time Charlie was offered a meal at his friends' home, but he always declined. 'No thanks,' he would say. 'They will be expecting me.' He knew his mother loved to feed him. Stomach filled, he would return to the Caldwells and help Willie or Hugh prepare the horse and carriage for their father's afternoon trip to nearby Three Chain Road (now Moorooduc) for his late service.

After watching Rev. Caldwell meander up and over the hill, the boys would go inside for a drink of tea and pack snacks for their weekly two or three-hour wander through the scrub or to dam the creek for eels, returning only when nightfall threatened.

Jim did not go on these trips, it seems. He was more likely to stay at home and talk to his mother or sister. Often they would gossip about other families or discuss the town's latest development.

The train line to Mornington had been finished in 1889 after much lobbying of Melbourne-based politicians by leading citizens. On the day of the grand opening, the new station platform and the entire town were decorated in flags and ribbons in 'quite a gay appearance'. Hundreds of people gathered at the terminus to watch as carriages came filled with pollies, greeted by a grinning president and councillors of the shire. The most senior government minister, Dr Charles Henry Pearson, was driven around town before being delivered to the Mechanics' Institute for a banquet, attended by eighty gentlemen. Dr Pearson probably assumed most of the locals were friendly.

Shire President Alfred Downward hosted the dinner and proposed toasts before inviting Dr Pearson to speak. The Member of Parliament congratulated the people of Mornington on the 'opening for traffic of the line railway'. The drink was flowing and the crowd was starting to tingle when Dr Pearson began waffling on about his latest political project (to oppose undenominational Bible instruction in state schools). The audience clapped politely. The guest of honour concluded by saying Australia was, 'one of the greatest nations upon the globe'.

Local Member of the Legislative Council, Hon. Frank Dobson, then made his address to the banquet, apologising for his 'nasal' speech (he had a cold), and declared Mornington's newest ambition should be to 'bring the beautiful township within the suburban radius' of Melbourne. Everyone listening knew he was proposing trains on Sundays.

More men spoke. There was a representative of the Legislative Assembly and the shire council. Then came the most interesting speaker of the day: Reverend James Caldwell.

Smoke filled the room. Rev. Caldwell, with long, distinguished whiskers, introduced himself as a proud Irishman. The crowd cheered and raised their drinks. He said he had been a resident of Mornington for fifteen years. A bigger cheer went up.

'I have taken a personal interest in the Mornington railway,' he went on. 'Also in other improvements, and in my opinion, Mornington is the prettiest place on the shores of the bay and the queen of Victorian watering places.'

The room filled with adulation for his stirring speech.

Then came a change. Rev. Caldwell, without altering demeanour, said personally he dissented from the 'expressed hope of some of the previous speakers in reference to Sunday trains'.

The audience paused to see if a joke was coming. When it didn't, some of the listeners gave a light 'booooo'.

'What's more, I'll do all in my power to oppose the running of Sunday trains to Mornington,' said the Presbyterian minister, ignoring the rising dissent.

'They could keep their train at Frankston,' he added

in defiance. 'We do not want the riff raff of Melbourne at Mornington.'

Before he left the stage he offered Dr Pearson a stiff challenge that schools should have Bible instruction, of course they should. It was a bold and defiant display of the man's character.

When the gentlemen later adjourned for a ball, joined by ladies in elegant lace dresses, in the corners of the hall built by funds raised from a committee Rev. Caldwell chaired, they no doubt talked about the speech he had given. It was the most remarkable anyone could recall.

Gone was the 'gay appearance' when Charlie Allchin made it home on the train in 1891. The station hadn't been upgraded or even maintained for two years and was filthy. He grabbed his bags from the wire luggage net and hustled off the carriage, saying hello to the familiar stationmaster. Charlie strode from the platform behind Main Street and passed few people on the way to his parents' home. The town was so very quiet. And it worried him.

Thirteen

Sarah did not greet Charlie at the door, as she usually did; rather, the gardener's wife met him with the news that half the population of the district was sick.

'Where's Mother?'

'She's in bed.'

Sarah Allchin was now elderly, much unlike the woman who had arrived to make her mark on Schnapper Point in the 1850s. Charlie's parents now lived without their children. The eldest son, Tom, had moved to Queensland. Descendants who have researched their family heritage believe Thomas wanted Tom to follow him into construction, but Tom didn't want to. They clashed and Tom moved to the town of Rockhampton, thousands of kilometres away.

Charlie's sisters had married and lived in Mornington. Emmie wed a successful farmer, Robert Olley, of the 'Clydebank' property, and Ella married prominent solicitor

William Sym Cook. In 1889, Cook's father, Archibald, famous owner of the Yarra River's first ferry service, hired J. D. Grover (and his apprentice Hugh Caldwell) to build Ella and William a brick and slate roof mansion called 'Morven', one of the town's best known homes. Two Norfolk pines were planted in the yard, the beginning of one of the peninsula's most attractive gardens. The manor was in the same street as Sarah and Thomas Allchin. Still, it made the matriarch sad not to have any of her four children living with her at Sutton Grange for the first time in more than thirty years. Worse, she now had the flu.

Charlie soon learned from his mother that his sister Ella had also been struck down. Charlie's father didn't have flu symptoms but was too old these days to act as a nurse. The Allchins never had servants so the gardener's wife had offered to stay close and do what she could.

From that second until the epidemic was over, Charlie stepped into the role as saviour, bringing food, water, medicine and kindness.

Surviving documents show the essence of Charlie's relationship with his family, particularly his mother. A descendant, Janet Groves, who still lives in the district and is a leading member of the Mornington and District Historical Society, is in possession of the letters, mostly from the 1880s, while Charlie was a weekly boarder at Wesley College.

Here is part of a letter, written from Wesley in 1888, three years before the flu outbreak. In short, he was still relying on his mother to take care of him.

Dear Mother

The trams are in full swing along St Kilda Road now. They run a great deal more regularly than the buses used to. The pocket in my silk coat caught on a nail on Saturday morning and tore so badly that I cannot wear it. These patched breeches are also starting to go at the knees. It is a nuisance not having a silk coat now that the hot weather has come. Could you make me a coat of the same flannel as they make cricket things out of, about the same size as that gray coat, only with a collar more like one of those on my night shirts? I don't mean a cricketing shirt. Some of the fellows have those sort of coats and they look just as well as silk coats to wear about the school or anywhere except church etc.

Charlie was always looking forward to his next hunting trip. He often brought friends back to the peninsula during longer holidays.

Please don't forget to send me up the dates of every full moon between now and March as Sam [a school friend] and I want to have a debate about the most suitable time to get out on that expedition of ours at Christmas.

I remain your affectionate son.

C E Allchin.

Charlie was straight-talking, ambitious and loving.

Letters to Charlie from his mother were often shorter. One from 1890, in the week of his eighteenth birthday, reinforces the place he had in her life.

My dear Charlie

God's word says the Blessing of the Lord maketh rich . . . Ask that you would see; this Blessing it is above the other treasures and does not hinder you from worldly prosperity only enables you to use this every gift without abusing them . . .

(This) is the birthday prayer of your loving mother.

S Allchin

Sarah Allchin was the strictest of Wesleyans, a founding member of the Mornington Abstinence Society (from 1865). Her membership card read:

I voluntarily promise to abstain from all intoxicating Drinks, except for Medical purposes and Religious Ordinances.

One of the Bible extracts on the membership card warns:

'Wine is the mocker: strong drink is raging: and whosoever is deceived thereby is not wise.' – Prov. XX. 1.

To those outside the Allchin family Sarah was a 'quiet, unassuming woman' and Charlie was 'the light of his mother's eye'. Now he wanted to repay her love by nursing her back to health. He would spend as long as it took to care for her and his sister, as well as one other.

The next day Charlie went to visit Hugh, who was among the sick. It would have been alarming to anyone to see one of the fittest lads in town without colour and movement, sweating and heaving through the fever. But for Charlie it was even more distressing. His friend could die.

So began perhaps Charlie Allchin's finest weeks. All day,

every day, his boots wore a path from Sutton Grange to Main Street, for stores, and over to the Caldwell house, before going back to his mother's side, stopping by Morven when he had time. He spent his days checking temperatures, making sure medicines were taken, saying something cheery to adjust morale.

On stopping by the Caldwells, he would race up the stairs to Hugh's room, take a look at his mate and curse the doctor for not making him well. Then, down he'd go to the kitchen to see if he could help strain jellies or prepare some other soft food, making conversation with the staff. After half an hour – and no longer – he would tell Hugh he was off and head out the front door to complete his rounds.

His tenderness during this period left a mark on all the locals. It confirmed in Hugh, as he slowly regained health, that he had a dear mate.

Fourteen

The Depression was worsening. Small building societies were collapsing. Overseas investors had stopped spending in Australia. Commodity prices were falling. The major banks were feeling only the beginning of their earthquake. Unemployment, disease, hunger, fear, suicide and sadness loomed like storm clouds yet to properly break.

One weekly activity brought excitement and relief to the start of this decade of doom. Some say football is a reflection of life. More often, it is a distraction *from* life.

Trying to beat Frankston had become Mornington's chief aim and frustration. The competition between the towns' teams, though not old, was maturing into something thrilling, funny and spiteful.

Players and barrackers on both sides had come to think of their competition as akin to Australia's most famous rivalry: Sydney versus Melbourne. Victorians didn't like the attitude of people from New South Wales, considering those north of the border a bunch of posers, always talking up their role as 'Mother colony', as well as their harbour. Mornington folk, when the comparison came up, said they played the role of Melburnians: industrious, friendly and fair. Frankston people were all-the-way Sydneysiders, 'hoarding their advantages' – larger population and better sporting teams – and giving Melbourne nothing but putdowns.

At this time, Frankston had beaten Mornington with ease from 1887 to the end of 1890, a year that saw Frankston play ten games, winning eight, drawing two, kicking forty-five goals and conceding only five.

However, Mornington was improving and openly declaring it wanted to claim the district's unofficial 'premiership'. This riled the champion Frankston mob.

One day Willie Caldwell was caught in the middle of this seaside village rivalry. He did not provoke the attack and he could not fathom it. Willie was as intelligent as any of his teammates and by now was training to become a doctor. But he was sometimes a bit slow to catch on in social situations. He was also, for some unknown reason, a common target for personal insult from barrackers prone to tormenting opposition players.

It was the first game of the 1891 season. Mornington and Frankston had walked onto the field under full sun before the largest football crowd yet assembled in this and neighbouring shires. The audience was filled with anxious hometown Frankston supporters, including one man who shouted, 'Hello, HELLO . . .!'

His greeting (or was it a question?) was for Willie. 'So they had to get you down from the mighty Scotch College to help them?'

Willie was known to have played matches for Scotch, though perhaps not many because he was never an official member of the First Twenty. He was now playing occasionally for his new college, Ormond, which was attached to Melbourne University. But the big-voiced man didn't know details; he only understood another Caldwell on the team sheet was a boon for Mornington.

'But we have got as good players as you any day and a mighty side better,' the barracker went on. 'And you guys are not going to win this game, I can tell you.'

Others joined in, targeting Willie with taunts. Willie stayed silent, refusing to fan the sparks. He was the son of a gentleman and it would not be manly to respond to comments from what his father would call the riff-raff.

By now it was a rare match that hosted two Caldwells. Hughie would always turn out, but Jim had recently moved to live in Tasmania with Tom. Willie came home infrequently. Most Saturdays he spent in the city, looking for fun with his university friends. This was one of the few matches he could be talked into playing.

'Come down and help us do Frankston,' Hugh requested in a telegram. 'You must know we will need you!'

Willie liked to be needed. On the field, he spat on his hands to make them stickier, and stood ready to take a leap and mark the ball if it came his way.

Fifteen

The matches in 1891 would have a tension that didn't exist in earlier seasons. Back in 1888 the games had the atmosphere of a family Christmas Day: merriment with the odd spat. Match reports were generous and bright:

> The day was fine and the attendance, especially the ladies, good, and it was generally anticipated that the Mornington team would on this occasion retrieve the laurels, but the young lady – Miss Fortune – still clings to them, and the Frankston players secured two goals to nil, after some exciting play.

In 1889 expectations at The Point were higher but a typhoid epidemic in May made winning and losing irrelevant, as families tried to keep loved ones alive. Health spokesmen implored residents to 'properly and regularly remove all refuse matter', clean gutters and sweep drains, minding not to leave it in a pile, and to boil water and milk. Some

Saturday afternoon activities were suddenly more critical than leather chasing.

But the season did go on. And Mornington found no joy at the end of any games against Frankston, the team wearing red and black.

By 1890 the Frankston Football Club had become the slick-haired kid in the schoolground, blowing smoke rings at classmates during recess. On 12 April, the *Mornington Standard* published a note sent to the paper by a Frankston official, stating the team's record was 28 wins from 38 matches (with four draws). It was a challenge to the other teams to come and try your luck against the *best*. Jack Sadleir was still captain. Any country team with Sadleir on side would be confident.

Mornington started 1890 well by flogging Hastings five goals to one. Then came Frankston. By now, Mornington's ambitions had firmed.

Before the next game an accord was reached between clubs that only residents or recent residents of towns could represent their teams. A tactic was creeping into football that saw accomplished players who lived elsewhere brought into the district for one-off matches. It was a form of cheating. Most teams had tried it.

The *Standard* noted at the beginning of the nineties: 'Both clubs have agreed to play only local men, the match will be won and lost on its merits.'

The accord was broken when Frankston arrived in Mornington with only sixteen players and had to recruit a couple of its supporters and two men who happened to be visiting from Hastings. Soft rain floated in from clouds drifting across Port Phillip, soaking a big crowd with 'a fair quota of the fair sex'.

Sadleir won the toss and kicked off. (They were still kicking the ball off the ground to start matches, a rule that would change to a 'bounce down' next season.) Minutes later the Frankston skipper assisted one of his teammates to kick the first goal. Another followed. The lead was two. But Mornington scored next, the eye-popping fifteen-year-old Hugh Caldwell showing speed and a fine boot. The record would state a goal was 'nicely kicked by Caldwell'.

Goals became impossible in the second half because the field was of mud and the ball felt as heavy as a bluestone. Wrestling took the place of football and it became a violent spectacle. Frankston's fear of losing was visible when Sadleir called play to stop, declaring he would refuse to continue until the umpire promised to be fairer in awarding free kicks.

This must have been a shock to everyone. Until now Sadleir had been a man apart, a footballer with high-level experience, a gentleman banker and leader. Quibbling with a volunteer umpire (whose name does not appear in any match reports) could be seen as beneath Jack Sadleir. Anyway, his interjection apparently worked. Play resumed and he was satisfied thereafter his team wasn't being dudded. The cowbell sounded and his team had won by a goal.

Mornington looked forward to the rematch but had to wait a couple of weeks. In between, South Brighton and Dromana became scalps.

The next local derby rolled around. Reported the *Standard*:

> 'Barrackers' were there in full force from the boy who can just kick his hat, to the old grey-haired veteran whose delight it seems to watch the 'boys' indulging in this most favourite pastime.

Predictably, the hint of ring-ins (some players were now apparently being paid match fees) influencing results had sparked the bookmakers' interest. Bookies, dressed in long coats with wide pockets, were in the audience this day and at every popular match from then. Bets ran in favour of Mornington.

The game ended in a draw, one goal for each team.

Once again Sadleir asked for the match to be stopped for an umpiring protest. It seemed a game could no longer pass without controversy and complaints.

Despite the flimsy agreement to stop cheating, hired guns continued to be recruited by teams, or at least that was the repeated allegation. Take this game between Mornington and Hastings (1890) as an example of how two teams saw the same infringement in different shades of dodgy, depending on which side of the peninsula they called home.

This match report published in the *Standard* came from the pen of a Mornington 'correspondent':

> The local boys played a splendid game of football on Saturday last. Although at the outset it looked as if the match was going to fall through, seeing that the Hastings club had such a lot of foreign players. This should not be allowed and strong efforts ought to be made by those interested with the clubs, to play only members of such clubs. The game ended in a draw each side kicking one goal.

In the same publication, the Hastings club reported:

> On Saturday last our footballers played the Mornington team. Considerable time was lost owing to the objections raised by the Mornington players against some of the Hastings men, who had been invited to make up the team, so that it was 4 o'clock before the start was made. After a severe and well contested game, during which good play was shown on both sides, the result was a draw.

The Hastings club admitted it had 'invited' players from outside to represent the town. Its only gripe was that Mornington made an issue of it. The press published a letter on the next page, written by an anonymous Hastings supporter calling himself 'Disgusted'.

> The game was fast and furious from the kick off, and resulted in a draw. The scores being one goal each. I might say in conclusion that the Mornington showed a very selfish spirit by objecting to the composition of the Hastings team, when you take into consideration of the fact that if the visitors were erring in that direction they [Mornington] were equally as much to blame for bringing players from the other districts. I would also like to express an opinion as to the ability of the umpire, his umpiring being something to be remembered by the visitors, no doubt he did his best as far as his knowledge of the game would allow, but I am afraid that as far as football is concerned his education has been sadly neglected and would advise him if he wishes to continue in that line to take a trip to Metropolis, and see the game as it is now played.

Offence was taken. A Mornington committeeman wrote the following week:

> In the match alluded to, he characterises the conduct of the central umpire in rather satirical terms . . . Well, Mr Editor, as a follower of the game for the past 14 years. . . I felt rather grieved. It appears to me that this narrow minded man is allowed to abuse everybody with whom he comes in contact with impunity, but as he is well known to one and all of the local team, I shall treat him and his writings as an object beneath my observations.

Mornington's 1890 soured after the narrow loss and draw to Frankston was followed by the whinging of the Hastings affair. A third local derby saw Frankston win again, this time three goals to nil. By the time a fourth match was scheduled in late spring, The Point's public enthusiasm for football had withered. Mornington could not even field a full team. Frankston, not wasting its sympathies, and reinforcing its 'Sydney' reputation, handed Mornington its worst loss nine goals to one.

But by the first clash of the 1891 season (notwithstanding the Rovers' match), Mornington had trained properly and made sure it had a strong team, meaning Willie Caldwell, among others, travelled from the city to be there for his brother Hugh and his teammates.

Sixteen

Willie was not initially aggrieved by the crowd's abuse toward him. The minute before a game of football, particularly one that *matters*, like a final or a grudge match, is the most tantalising of all. The butterflies that have been in the stomach all morning have fluttered away. Adrenaline takes over, bumps the heart rate up a beat, gives players goosebumps, and calms them all at once. Minds start imagining that first collision.

The cowbell sounds.

The umpire bounced the ball to start the game. Both teams charged in at each other. Frankston took the ball away from the first scrimmage and scored quickly. Locals cheered with pride and, quite possibly, a measure of arrogance. Hats were thrown into the air and the home side relaxed, perhaps thinking another victory was its right.

Sadleir took a mark near goal but missed, an action he repeated in the second quarter. That was odd, onlookers thought. Not to worry. Frankston scored another goal and led by two at half-time. A few minutes after the half-time rest, the locals kicked another goal. Three goals down, it was looking a miserable day for all who'd travelled from The Point.

The crowd started in again on Willie. The same abuse that didn't penetrate before the game burrowed under his skin when his team was losing. He shouted back at one of the hecklers.

'Don't you think that you could borrow a telephone, and connect it with the telegraph wires, and then, perhaps, you might communicate your remarks to the inhabitants of Collins Street, for they really have no interest for me.'

It was an attempt to remain dignified but it cast him as a snob. Some of the Frankston children started walking onto the field, echoing their parents' insults. Willie shook his head and muttered something about 'ill bred' kids. Once he turned and ran at them. They scattered and then came back at him.

He wished his eleven-year-old brother Jack was there. Willie's family later recalled him saying, 'My word, Jack. I wish that I had had you there this afternoon. You would have kept those cheeky youngsters at arm's length; they roared at me until my head ached, but what could I do? I could not box their ears, they were too small; and if I turned and pretended that I was going for them they fled like hares, though they were back again the next minute, knowing, of course, that I would not hurt them.'

'Do you think I could have fought them?' asked little Jack, who had some competitive Hughness in him.

'I do not mean fight them, just keep them at a respectable distance,' Willie said. 'They would have been too frightened to tackle you, knowing that I was there. They are jolly little curs, I am sure, or they would never have gone on as they did today.'

To a neutral observer, it seemed unusual for Willie to be singled out. He was only eighteen but six feet one with a soldier's posture. Yet the children weren't scared to 'get on to him'. Only his siblings might say it was not surprising Willie would be under fire. Once, Jim Caldwell said, 'I never saw such a rum card as old Bill. Wherever he goes, the youngsters make a set at him. They never do it to me and yet, you know, strangers often mistake us for one another.'

The real reason the children acted that way was they were mimicking their elders. And that day at Frankston, there was fear they were not far enough in front. At half-time, the game wasn't yet won.

They were right to be worried.

Momentum changed in the third quarter. Maybe it was the late-autumn heat, or perhaps the Frankston boys were not as fit as they thought. Or it could have been that Mornington players just took a half to feel comfortable with each other. Whatever the cause, the result was a third quarter belting. All the play was in front of Frankston's goal (Mornington's scoring end). The locals could not run it away and eventually Mornington kicked a goal courtesy of a man called G. Bellairs. He then notched a second and the bank manager Henry Short, an ace goal sneak, just missed another. The crowd started to go berserk. The press later reported:

> When the last term was entered upon the excitement was intense, the barracking being something to remember.

One of Mornington's best players was captain James Wall. He took a little mark, shot for goal, and through it went. Throats in the crowd must have been sore from shouting. The board read three goals each, with Frankstonites becoming 'wilder and wilder'. Willie and Hugh Caldwell, and the entire Mornington team, sensed a win.

When a top team that doesn't believe it can lose is stretched to the point where it is possible, it becomes very careful, a perilous footballing state of mind.

Finally, Mornington's moment came. The bankman Short picked the spilt ball from the grass, brought it up to his groin and then dropped it back down again, kicking it with his toe the moment it pecked the turf. The ball went bullet-like through for a goal.

Later it would be labelled 'a grand kick'.

The ball was near Mornington's goal when the bell was rung. The visitors had been brilliant in victory. Willie waved to the crowd and walked to shake hands with the other team after 'one of the best contested games ever played in the district'. Frankston whined in the press but not without some sportsmanship.

> The visitors thus succeeded in defeating the Frankston on their own ground for the first time and therefore are to be congratulated but had they strictly played with their own men the victory would have been doubly meritorious. They deserve

> great credit for the plucky and uphill game they fought and each and all played in good form.

The two teams would play three more times that year; not all contests would end so amicably.

Seventeen

A river called the Meander flows through northern Tasmania, right where its heart might be, from mountain bluffs called the Great Western Tiers down through the modest towns of Westbury and Deloraine, once home to wealthy farmers and soft, Irish-green grass.

This country is part of the Caldwell story. It was where Tom and Jim settled after they left Mornington. Landing here was no fluke. The brothers' aunts, uncles and cousins, from their mother's side, lived on large parcels of land. The inheritance of their grandfather William Lindsay stretched across many acres.

Tom Caldwell was the first Victorian grandson of the late Hobart Town victualler to take up his calling. In the late 1880s, after his three-year stint at Scotch College, he told his father of his plans. Leave was granted and Tom made contact with his mother's sisters to say he was coming. Two of them had married into the wealthiest clan in the colony – the

Field family, which owned much of northern Tasmania – and were now living in luxury along the Meander's banks.

The patriarch of the Fields was the late William Field, an ex-convict who became a pastoralist and Launceston region meat supplier, one of the richest men in the history of the state.

One of Tom's aunties, Elizabeth Lindsay, had married William Field's son – Thomas William Field – and lived in a Georgian palace called 'Westfield'. Thomas Field went on to become a politician (The Honourable Thomas William Field MLC), and bred pure cattle and sheep.

Elizabeth's sister Mary Ann Lindsay then married Thomas Field's brother John, who owned a property called 'Calstock' near Deloraine. John Field bred racehorses and prepared the 1884 Melbourne Cup winner Malua, Australia's most versatile all-distance champion.

The Lindsay sisters and their Field husbands lived only ten miles apart and had more than twenty children between them. Most of them were still living in the district when Tom Caldwell came to settle. He must have felt quite special entering into the realm of this relatively royal family.

Jim Caldwell was in Melbourne at this point, having started a 'mercantile life', employed as a junior clerk at Australian Alliance Insurance in Collins Street. He was boarding with some other young men at his father's Hope Terrace apartments in East Melbourne. It wasn't a hard life. He was not paying rent and was being well looked after. He called his accommodation 'the Diggings'. Among the boarders lived an older woman, Mrs Philp, who acted as a servant. Jim was her favourite, or so the other boarders claimed.

'I hope you don't mind, Mr Caldwell,' Mrs Philp would

say to Jim. 'But this afternoon I had nothing else to do, so I took the liberty of going to your drawers to see if there were any socks there that wanted mending.'

'There you are,' Jim said once, feigning annoyance. 'A fellow can't call a chest of drawers his own in this place.'

Jim didn't have too many of those lighter moments in the city. His health was faltering because he was homesick. Rev. Caldwell was moved to take Jim to see a doctor, who found no disease. The doc just suggested Jim head back to Mornington for a while and breathe the fresher air.

His advice to Jim's father was, 'Take him home and let him amuse himself with a barrow and spade, about your own garden for a while, and he will grow into a fine strong lad.'

Jim quit his job in Melbourne, receiving a silver watch chain and locket from his colleagues, went back to The Point and ailed no longer.

His next career move came after Tom invited him to Tasmania to help at his property, 'Eaglehawk'. Jim packed up his belongings and cleared out. He told his family he would be back in about eighteen months. All who knew Jim worried for him. Of all the Caldwell brothers, he was perceived as the most fragile. If he could not stand life in Melbourne, with all its modern advances, how could he prosper clearing earth in the extreme temperatures of Tasmania? Perhaps Jim asked his reflection the same question. But he went anyway.

Tom greeted Jim at Launceston in the cooling month of May. The pair drove to Eaglehawk. Jim first saw its beauty and knew his physical task was as large as the old trees he would have to chop down. Tom told him the soil was rich.

All they had to do was clear the property and they could start sowing crops.

Winter proved the longest season and the Caldwell boys slept in a tent for longer than they had planned because rain had ruined the roads and no timber could be hauled in to make their house. During some of those earliest nights, when the campfire relaxed to ashes, the brothers nearly froze. In daytime, they fought back against the weather and country, cutting trees to the ground and setting them alight. They were never cold again and Jim's health, far from wilting, improved. Correspondence between Jim and his family back in Mornington was constant during these few months, despite the flu epidemic that had floored Hugh and Sarah Allchin and so many others. The letters sent to Jim across Bass Strait were fumigated by eucalyptus oil to prevent germs travelling. Inside the envelope was 'wadding', also soaked in oil.

Jim made mentioned of the smell on the envelope in a letter back home. In this paragraph is evidence of his mood.

> By the bye, the next time you write, send me some of that scent you put on the notepaper. It had the most delightful smell, very like what you get coming down the Yarra.

His family may not have been able to see his face but they could tell he was happy.

Tom gave Jim the job of cook, over coals outside the tent and in the kitchen of the four-room house, a building made in haste after the roads firmed. His best dishes had potatoes in them. Visitors often said his spuds, as light as balls of flour, would 'warm an Irishman's heart'.

The Field aunties and cousins would call in to see the Caldwell boys at work and stay for dinner. After a course of meat and potatoes Jim always served bread and butter, with as much tea as the visitors could drink, boiled in a tin teapot over the hob. He did not bake cakes or pudding. The treats came from the cooks at the Calstock mansion.

Over meals Jim and Tom made sure they showed the Fields they were gentlemen, even though they had made a bachelors' home. Once, a relaxed cousin attempted to spread butter on bread with a knife that had been used to slice meat. 'Hullo, there,' Jim said, reaching for a drawer under the tablecloth to find another knife for his relative. 'We don't use the same knives for everything here.'

Caldwell family history has it that Tom and Jim were the original Odd Couple. Jim was the neat one, always resting his boots and spurs in the same place, and careful to leave a clothes brush where he could find it (usually face up on the rabbit skin covering his chest of drawers). Tom left his boots where he took them off, and did not own a clothes brush. Of course, if he wanted use of one, Jim's would do. As Jim explained in one of his letters:

> I am used to it now. I don't mind. The poor old chap is always in such a hurry. It is the same with everything. Sometimes I go into my room and find drawers pulled out, and socks all over the place. It does not take me long to find what has been going on. Tom suddenly finds that he had to go to the township, so he goes up to the house to make himself presentable, finds his socks are damp when he goes to change his boots, goes to his drawers – no socks there. Stumps off into my

room. Pulls out the drawers and sits down on my bed trying to put on my socks, which are not stretched to his size, over his damp feet. The consequence is he had undone about half a dozen pairs before he gets two out of the lot on, and finally starts off with odd socks on his feet, and the rest of mine all over the place.

The manual labour made both brothers powerful. Like most men freed of their suits and ties, Jim enjoyed feeling his hands and shoulders firming. They were axe men, who sharpened their blades each day. The tightness in his limbs and the toughening of his skin was evidence he was growing up faster in this wild place than he could ever have done with Mrs Philp mending his socks. At the end of each workday, the Caldwells would sit and drink cup after cup of tea until the kerosene lamps ran low. Then they slept like tired children after a day at the beach.

After the farm was cleared and started producing vegetables, the brothers decided to hire help. A married couple with children had come looking for work. Tom and Jim said the wife could maintain order in the house if the husband became their labourer. It worked at first. The house was kept as well as it ever would be. Jim wrote in a letter to Mornington:

> This place is getting spoiled. In fact, a fellow might as well be in town, as the woman here actually makes the beds and scrubs the floors and sweeps the rooms out, and puts away all the clothes you leave about, and finished up on Saturday night by cleaning your best boots for Sunday.

The married couple experiment only failed in the end because they had 'spirited' kids. The children were too noisy and Jim found it hard to write his letters in peace. Also, the little ones played with the axes. The couple was sacked before their children lost their fingers or toes. Tom next employed an old, one-eyed man to act as servant. 'Old Jock' woke up before the sun and made his bosses' breakfast every morning, cooking potatoes to save the bread. His favourite line was, 'Eat plenty of potatoes . . . they are the things to work on.'

Old Jock kept his gun loaded, leaning against the wall beside the kitchen door. If he saw a hawk hovering over the chickens in the yard he would take his gun and look up into the sky . . . shoot . . . and probably miss. The brothers, swinging axes, running the plough, or sipping tea in the paddock, would laugh at the boom and echo: sounds of their wonderful new life.

Eighteen

It was nearly midnight in Mornington. A man with wide shoulders and a smooth, moonlit face was walking past houses a block from Main Street. Curiously, he was carrying a bag. It was Hugh Caldwell.

The teenager turned left from the road and went into the Allchin property, past the house with the brick tower, all the way to the stables. On opening the door he looked inside; there was Charlie, sitting by the slowest pulse of a dying candle.

What Hugh said to Charlie is not recorded. But the language between young men was no more complicated in colonial days than it is now. All they needed was a look, smile or nod – maybe a word or two.

'Did you get them?' Charlie might have asked.

Yes.

From his bag, Hugh lifted two candles and lit one of them. The stable walls and ceiling now illuminated, Hugh and Charlie went back to building the skeleton of a boat.

The idea had come to Hugh while he was recovering from the flu. It was an enticing challenge. No first-time boat builders were better prepared for the job. Charlie, the trainee architect, had drawn the plans. Hugh had sourced the materials and was to build it. Together they could shape a nautical future.

At first, they had kept the project between them because they didn't want their parents to warn them off it. And they wanted to see how it turned out before the unveiling.

Keeping it secret from Charlie's parents, however, was impossible. Sarah and Thomas would have wondered why their son was coming home on weekends from Melbourne only to sit in the stables all Saturday and Sunday nights (in winter and spring he arrived home on Saturday afternoons, sometimes to play football, and went back to Melbourne on the Monday morning train). Even if Charlie was capable of lying to his mother, and it's hard to believe, Sarah would have had to ask what Hugh was up to when he started popping around on weekdays to cut and hammer timber among the animals. So Charlie successfully asked his father for permission. And soon Hugh told his little brother Jack and sisters Jeannie and Sallie. Alice noticed candles missing from the storeroom, but that was all. She would find out along with everyone else what a disastrous vessel her brother and his mate had been making.

Nineteen

By now, Mornington and Frankston had played each other three times during the 1891 season. Both teams had won a game, with a draw in-between. The final match of the season was about to take place.

After Mornington won that first game, Frankston's members and supporters had counted the days until the rematch. But there were other teams to consider. The advent of the Rovers became an interesting subplot to the neighbouring towns' rivalry.

In short, the Mornington breakaway team was the most enigmatic on the peninsula. At best they matched it with Frankston, at worst they didn't even turn up. As the season went on, some Rovers players were included in the original Mornington team and vice versa. The class divide was often forgotten when it came time to regularly field two teams.

This was the case when Mornington hosted Frankston for their second match. On the same day, the Rovers were supposed to go by carriage across the peninsula to Flinders. The sport-loving Flinders minister Rev. W. L. Morton had lent his team a section of his property for an oval. But the Rovers telegraphed on the Friday to say they had 'no conveyance' to bring them to Flinders and wanted to postpone the match indefinitely.

Flinders players and supporters were miffed. A subsequent note was sent for the Rovers to contemplate.

> Seeing that this match was arranged some six weeks ago, it surely was not very considerate to send such an excuse at the last minute, as the Flinders team is so scattered that some of them did not hear the postponement, and turned up to find some equally disappointed spectators.

The truth was that a few of the Rovers players had committed to representing the Mornington club. The rest wanted to stay in town and watch. It was a big game, after all.

Frankston players arrived for their second encounter with Mornington aboard a horse-drawn carriage they called 'Millard's drag and four' (Millard was one of the players). It was their weekly ritual to shun train travel in favour of a slower, more social trip to matches. They liked to sing songs and tell jokes as they dodged potholes.

The crowd that turned up to watch was larger than the first game. 'Enthusiastic admirers' were dozens deep beyond the field. Almost all had wet shoes and socks following a week of deluges. The oval surface was soft and uneven.

Sadleir captained the visitors and he seemed particularly serious at the toss, which he won. The umpire, Senior

Constable Tom Murphy, bounced the ball in the middle but it didn't go any higher than his head and the game stalled from a crash of players around him. Instant mud fight. Teeth were clenched. Arms were locked. Heads clashed. Legs swung. Men swore murder. The ball was a prisoner under bodies. It was going to be a bloody slog.

Frankston scored the first goal after a clever mark and kick. Then the ball was carried down the other end and . . .

'What a mark!'

Hugh Caldwell had seized the ball cleanly from its flight. He lined up and kicked a 'neat' goal for the home side. Hats flew high. Then one of the Rovers men – a twenty-one-year-old fisherman called Francis Foss – proved his value by kicking a goal off the ground, English football-style.

Strength was needed in the congestion of bodies and a young player was proving himself made for the weather.

'Who *is* that?'

The mud was already masking identities.

It was Willie Coles. Like Hugh, he had been a stand-out athlete in Mornington for a few years. He was also a leading musician, member of the popular town brass band that had formed the previous year. Coles was known for playing his cornet and singing at concerts, often winning stand-up applause.

His full name was William Henry Coles and he was the son of Englishman James John Coles, the Main Street blacksmith, who had married Emma Worrell. The Coles had seven children, although one died in infancy in 1876. Willie was his parents' eldest and excelled at everything he did, including his job as blacksmith and wheelwright in his father's business.

He had played a lot of cricket but this was his first game of football against Frankston and he was showing what a fillip he was to his town's hopes. He was described as the 'heaviest boy' on the team. His weight was in his backside, chest and shoulders. If he were a racehorse they'd have said he was suited to a dead track.

The visitors pressed to level the score but kicking was becoming problematic because of the dreadful state of the ground. Every time someone plucked the ball and surged for freedom from tacklers, the ground moved under his boots. Slipping was dangerous. Tired players are most likely to whack you in the head, from clumsiness and frustration.

'Keep your pucker up!' a supporter who had travelled with the Frankston team called out. Apparently such encouragement worked. The record says Frankston 'bucked in with determination'.

Mornington needed men to grab the ball and charge with it up the other end. Charles Hooper was a top defender this day. At thirty-four, the well-known fisherman was the old man of the team. He had the best handlebar moustache and was admirably balanced, no doubt earned from a lifetime at sea. By his side in protecting the Mornington 'citadel' were the goal-sneak Henry Short, sensing danger at the end most foreign to him, and Alfred Lawrence, yet another newcomer, known to onlookers as the boy who worked in his father's general store. Leading all these blokes was the 'follower' Tom Coxhell. (Followers were players with roaming or 'roving' commissions.) Coxhell, a baker, was sinewy and tackled like a guard dog.

Time fell away and the crowd became desperate.

Mornington led two goals to one but were not in command. There were echoes of the Mornington-Rovers derby in the voices of the audience, the 'crowd exerting the players to increased efforts'. Frankston might have frozen when pressured last time but a top team doesn't seize up twice in a row. Sadleir was one of the saviours. Also, a man named Jimmy.

The *Standard* described the next minute of play.

> It now looked as if Frankston would be unable to equalize matters, but when Sadleir marked to Jimmy every breath was hushed. Although Jimmy was nearly 50 yards away on a difficult angle he was equal to the occasion and with a magnificent kick sent the ball flying through the posts this (sic) making the game even.

The bell rang. The final score was: Frankston 2 goals 7 behinds, Mornington 2 goals 3 behinds. Behinds were recorded but not yet used to determine a winner. A draw was declared.

The umpire was praised for being 'very fair'.

It stung the Mornington team to know it had missed a chance to win again and go to an unbeatable series lead. Still, a draw was okay. It meant the boys from The Point needed to win only one of the two remaining local derbies to take the premiership.

The annual concert was celebrated that night with gusto. Charlie Allchin couldn't make it down for the game but his sister Ella represented the family with distinction on the pianoforte. A full-tilt rendition of 'God Save the Queen' ended the night, which raised sixteen pounds.

A month later it was back to Frankston for game three. Winter was in its stride and the bay breeze seemed to be coming via Bass Strait. Mornington was now in love with the game and a huge convoy of vehicles brought a boisterous crowd.

Both teams had been strengthened. Frankston had included all its best players, and perhaps a couple of ring-ins. Locals were shocked to see some of its regular players on the side of the field in scarves and overcoats before the first bounce. Comments were passed on how strong the Frankston team would be today if such and such could not get a go. Three o'clock was the time to start. Sadleir again won the toss and chose to kick with the wind, hoping to build an imposing lead.

The umpire let fly and within a minute the home team scored a goal. The crowd gave a muted cheer. It wanted more goals before Mornington had the advantage of the wind, now almost a gale. The second celebration was louder when Frankston kicked its second goal a minute later.

Sadleir was in top form. With all his VFA experience he took a little mark and kicked a third goal for his team. He was inspiring his men.

Mornington scored a single goal, helped by the wind in the second quarter. Half-time score: Frankston 3 goals 4 behinds; Mornington, 1 goal 2 behinds. Still, the locals weren't jubilant. Mornington was still a 'good show' and could be expected to 'wear the locals out' in the last stages. It didn't happen that way. Frankston scored again and pressed for more.

Hooper and Willie Caldwell stopped most of the attacks. Willie was not badgered as he had been earlier that year.

Willie Coles and Henry Short were also drawn to defence, like firefighters to smoke. Tom Coxhell patrolled the middle of the field again with aplomb.

Even in the last quarter, down four goals to one, Mornington held hopes of a win but the wind had lost its force. Frankston scored again to make it five. Short, as he almost always did, snuck a goal past the home team defence but it was nowhere near enough. Frankston scored a sixth. The bell preceded a roar from the crowd. Order had been restored. Even the umpire didn't cop insults on the way off. One of the officials, as if to counter complaints from the crowd, showed Mornington players the free-kick count.

'You got more of them,' he said. 'See? Mornington sixteen and Frankston only fifteen.'

It was a trudge back to The Point.

Between game three and game four, there was a chance for the Rovers to play against Frankston one more time. Frankston barrackers noticed within minutes of the start that the Rovers had a lot of familiar faces. The farce of the Mornington-Rovers split was on display.

An official later wrote:

> No less than 11 players from Mornington played for the Rovers, including Short (who kicked three goals), Martin, Cavell, Coles, Coxshall, Hooper (2), Foster and Lawrence.

It didn't make any difference. Frankston, feeling invincible, won nine goals to four. The 'premiership' would be decided by Mornington versus Frankston in their fourth game of the season, scheduled for 22 August 1891. Venue: Mornington.

It was another frosty day, with spring yet to arrive. This time it was a line of vehicles coming the other way. At the head of the snake of carriages was the Frankston team, singing at the onlookers on Main Street, from Millard's drag and four, with red and black bunting.

The first controversy of the match came when Mornington unveiled two muscular recruits. Their names were Ernest Millman and Charles Droop, known to everyone as the two finest players ever to represent Mordialloc Football Club.

Frankston players knew Millman and Droop from previous outings and immediately accused Mornington of unsportsmanlike behaviour. Mornington officials explained to Sadleir that the Mordialloc pair had moved to The Point earlier that month to work as fishermen. A check of census documents from that year confirms Droop was, in fact, a fisherman. Millman was not.

Mornington countered accusations of cheating by alleging Frankston had drafted in a man called 'Brown' from Melbourne, and given him a match payment. Brown was apparently a former Frankston resident, who worked in the city, a similar situation to Willie Caldwell's. But Willie was an amateur, Mornington officials explained. So was Brown, Frankston said.

After such growling became childlike, Sadleir agreed to play against whichever team Mornington fielded. What else could he do? There was no time to cross-examine the Mordialloc men.

He won the toss, again, and went with the slight breeze. A quick goal was his reward but no more than that. In the second quarter, the part-time Rover Foss kicked a goal for Mornington to tie the scores. Then Frankston shot for another and Mornington claimed it hit the post but a goal was given. By now it was clear the game was going to be tight. Players were not being allowed by opponents to free themselves from scrimmages.

At half-time the scoreboard showed: Frankston 2 goals 3 behinds, Mornington 1 goal 3 behinds.

It had been a long, aching season and many of the players were carrying sore feet, legs, groins, shoulders and sprained fingers. Play was slow and violent. It was hard to score. In the end, it became impossible. Frequent were the sling tackles, head knocks, shin kicks, kidney slams, grappling, spitting, cursing, punching, and even head butting.

Willie Coles was targeted for 'rough play'. The visitors had three particularly aggressive players: Jimmy, Bentick and Kelso. Jimmy, a villain to the crowd that could not work out whether his name was his first or last, 'struck' Coles and twice 'slung' another youngster named Willie Robertson. This seemed like a revenge attack. Moments before, Robertson had picked the ball up and ran along the wing.

'He's distanced him there,' someone shouted in awe.

Kelso nabbed Robertson during a pause in play minutes later, grabbing him by the arm, using his bodyweight to catapult the faster man awkwardly. Not humbled by the taunts this attracted, Kelso went after the Mornington captain, William Martin, with a tackle that lifted him from the ground before slamming his body on the grass, the victim's head whiplashing, snot and spit spilling.

Paranoia and treachery ruined the second half and, really, the entire season. The closest anyone came to showing calm skill was when Henry Short took a shot and smiled as it was sailing through. Frankston players were shaking the post in desperation and Short's kick faded at the end, brushing the upright. The attempt was called a behind despite protests. Martin's boys were furious but played on. Soon they had another go at making scores level, when another player, the ringer Millman, shot straight for goal after taking a mark. However, the umpire (a man called Roberts, of Frankston, brought in because Senior Constable Murphy was busy policing), disallowed the score because the 'fisherman' had not kicked over his 'mark' (the man standing in the spot where the mark was taken). He was granted another attempt but missed the replay.

Frankston claimed victory. Hate was in the locals' eyes.

Among the best players for Mornington this day were Willie Coles, the new fishermen in town Droop and Millman, the old Rover Foss, Henry Short and the Caldwell brothers.

Frankston walked from the field with the umpire, later claiming he was 'strict and impartial'. That's not how the 'Pointites' saw it during the last quarter. Now they were nearly rioting. On instinct, both teams shook hands. The transgressions on the field often don't seem as unfair to participants as they do to the cold viewers. And it must be remembered that these combatants were not enemies. Some of them, including the captains Sadleir and Martin, played cricket together in a combined district team against Dandenong every summer. Sadleir always opened the batting with Mornington favourite J. D. Grover.

But after the handshakes came the accusations of dirty tricks from both teams. The Mornington crowd was incensed and threats of harm were hurled at the Frankston club and their umpire. The visitors, sensing there would be no genial post-match toast, boarded Millard's drag and headed for the town's nearest exit, at first singing (a song called 'We've Won the Victory'). This enraged their opposition and challenges were issued to play another game – game five! – at a neutral ground, at Hastings or Dromana, anywhere the result could not be corrupted.

Even the most passive Mornington residents hooted the winners as they passed. Then someone threw a stone, which should have shocked others into realising the rally had gone too far. But it did not. Others started throwing missiles – mud, sticks and more rocks. Sadleir's men fell silent, except to urge the driver to hurry up.

The aftermath of game four was not forgotten for a full summer. Nor was the match shrugged off. The battle for retrospective justice went where all sporting scandals go to die: the press.

A 'correspondent' wrote a week later in the *Standard*, in a column called 'Under the Ti-Tree'. First a defence of the umpire:

> The insinuation that Roberts was a partial umpire is also unjust for he is well known among footballers as an umpire of the strictest impartiality and having such a good record it is not likely that he would forfeit it to please either Frankston or Mornington.

Then an attack on Mornington:

> The simple fact is the Mornington boys cannot take a beating kindly, and their boast of meeting on neutral ground, etc. is all bluff, for they have been beaten too often to doubt which is the better team.

This was true. In four seasons the 'Mornington boys' had beaten their neighbours once.

> I may just here add, that it is a pity that these teams do not meet as others have met but to treat visitors on the last occasion, on leaving the township under a shower of mud and gravel, cannot be too strongly condemned and is contrary to all rules of hospitality and British fair play.

To leave the story of the 1891 series here would be to give Frankston the final word. Yet, all the published records belonged to Frankston authors and the fairer thing is to find a Mornington voice in this shouting match.

There was a letter published in the *Standard* on 10 September 1891. It came to the editor from Joseph Worrell, the former schoolmaster.

> Sir, - The reports in your journal are usually fairly given, and it is therefore a pity that you allowed to appear such a one-sided and incorrect report of the last Mornington and Frankston football match. I ask your permission to refer to a few points . . .

Worrell wrote about Frankston's roughness, naming culprits. Then he extended his list, not sparing Frankston's revered captain from criticism.

> Sadleir, Brown and Westaway . . . allowed their keenness to lead them to play a 'bullocking' game, and naturally other members of the team followed their example.

On the issue of ring-ins, Worrell covered old ground, as if he were a barrister summing up for the jury.

> The statement as to the Mornington importing Millman and Droop from Mordialloc is incorrect – the two players named, have been fishing here, off and on for some time and had been in the place for some weeks before the match, practicing with the locals, and still do so. This is a different version and not to be compared to Brown living in Melbourne, playing with Frankston and it is said having his expenses paid.

On a roll now, Worrell even tried to defend the indefensible.

> As to the crowd throwing stones and hooting the Frankston players, while admitting there can be no excuse for anyone throwing stones (if such really did occur) can anyone wonder at some outburst after the cowardly play of the players named, that the crowd many of whom had relatives and friends in the local team, and seeing them knocked about and injured by heavier men should hoot and groan – if ever football players did, the Frankston team did their level best to provoke a free fight and they can scarcely grumble at their song 'We've won

> the victory' being accompanied through the streets with the chorus of jeers and groans – And such a victory – for if ever a team were fairly and squarely beaten on their merits Frankston were on this occasion and they knew it too.
>
> Yours etc. J. E. Worrell.

A note accompanied this passionate letter. It came from the editor, who wrote and published it in Frankston. The afterword stated that its 'representative' (writer of the earlier report) was a Frankston player and witnessed all the events. The *Standard* concluded:

> We still adhere to the statements in our report of the 27th August.

The Mornington Football Club could not imagine a season ending as badly.

III

Racing Sails

Twenty

Hugh and Charlie had almost finished their not-so-secret boat. By now more people knew about the maritime project than didn't. Just the other day, one of the Caldwells' neighbours had called out to Hugh's stepmother, Marian, over the hedge, 'The boys will surely never go out in that boat they are building, until they let Mr Cook, or someone else that understands boats, see it.' The voice belonged to Elizabeth Cook, wife of Archibald Cook, the Yarra River's first ferryman. (He had also been a ship carpenter.) But neither Mr Cook nor any other qualified person inspected Hugh and Charlie's launch before it went into the harbour.

Wheeling the boat from the Allchins' Sutton Grange property to the jetty was tricky. Again, Charlie relied on his parents. An integral part of the Allchins' general store business was their goods boat, *Maggie*. The family employed an experienced sailor, Captain Jack Bunn, to sail *Maggie* to and from Melbourne almost every day. When Captain

Bunn wasn't running jobs for the Allchins he was hired out to others. His work, weaving between much bigger boats, sometimes on the busiest days, was often perilous. During the Easter weekend of 1884 the *Maggie* sank when it was accidentally rammed by the visiting steamer *Nelson*. Captain Bunn jumped into the water and was unhurt. But Sarah and Thomas suffered from the absence of a delivery service (the railway was still five years away). The incident was mentioned in letters passed down through the generations. This one was from Sarah to Charlie, who had been on a camping trip.

Sutton Grange
Mornington April 15/'84
My Dear Charlie
Yesterday (Easter Monday) there were two steamers in. One was the Nelson. She came rushing alongside the jetty and came into the crafts smashing the end of the Maggie and Captain of the Nelson would tug her up behind the Nelson and she went all right as far as we could see but this morning we got a telegram to say she had sunk off Rickett's Point. Poor old Maggie. I must close now with best love and hoping you will be a good boy and arrive home safe and well feeling the wiser for the sights you have seen.

Your affectionate Mother Allchin

In another note – from Sarah to her eldest son, Tom – she wrote 'the valuable tub' had to be fixed at great cost and the accident has caused her husband to not speak to her for weeks. It's unclear how the *Maggie*'s temporary demise was her fault.

In March 1891, six months before Hugh and Charlie tested their craft, Captain Bunn had another accident. He had sailed a load of hogsheads (barrels of beer) from Melbourne and lifted them onto his dray. After driving them to a local hotel, just up the hill from the jetty, he began unburdening the flat cart and one of the hogsheads fell on his right hand, tearing the 'flesh and sinews off . . . from the fingers and half way up the arm'.

Onlookers were sickened by the injury and Captain Bunn had to be rushed to the town's doctor to be stitched. His wound was still dressed by a bandage when Hugh and Charlie came to him looking to borrow his dray at the beginning of summer. The captain helped them wheel their creation to water's edge, noticing the boat had an oddly shaped hull.

The crowd gathering to watch the launch was bigger than the audience from the previous summer that had surrounded the brute of a stingray, five feet across with a three feet tail, caught off the jetty and dragged onto the pier.

All watched with trepidation as Hugh and Charlie boarded their unnamed vessel. Captain Bunn gave them a push. Immediately the lads could sense there was something wrong.

'We're too sharp in the keel,' Hugh said to Charlie, as they tried to balance.

The pair lolled around on ripples of waves for a few minutes, hoping they were wrong. But the boat was not well. They splashed back to the jetty. An argument followed. Hugh blamed Charlie for the design. 'I'll take good care to plan her myself next time,' he said. Charlie pointed out that any failure might have been in the making, not drawing.

However, closest mates don't argue for long. By the time they had the boat on land, they had agreed to pull her apart and remake her with a flat bottom.

Hugh knew they would require more timber and candles.

Twenty-one

While Hugh and Charlie spent the next month in the Allchin stables, Willie and Alice Caldwell went to visit Jim and Tom in Tasmania.

Jim had just celebrated his 21st birthday. Having overcome bouts of sickness as a youngster, he was now enjoying manhood. His visiting brother and sister noticed he had become tall (six feet one) and muscular (weighing thirteen stone); his forearms and hands bore the sheen of oiled cane.

Jim and Tom picked Alice and Willie up from Launceston and drove them back to their Eaglehawk homestead, laughing all the way. They passed an old Irish woman, whose son Jim knew as Mike. But she didn't like him being called Mike.

'And what for do you call my son Mike,' she asked. 'When his baptismal name is Michael John Joseph.'

'As if anyone is going to stay there half the day, while you thought out his baptismal names,' Jim later said. The Caldwell name gave some of the Irish tongues trouble in

Tasmania, causing pronunciation to vary. Some called Jim and Tom 'Mr Caudrover'. Alice liked to hear stories of the 'quaint' Irish. Another Irishwoman had asked Jim where he sourced his potato seeds. He said Melbourne. She said, 'I'm thinking of taking a walk over there myself in the spring.' Jim thought her a 'queer stick'.

Alice expected to see her brothers' bachelor home untidy but she found it as orderly as their Mornington manse (thanks to the one-eyed housekeeper Jock). There were things her brothers needed. Tom had bought a macintosh but it was too tight across his chest and he had popped the buttons. Jim had snared the coat.

'The boss doesn't want it anymore,' he told Alice, asking her to sew the buttons back on.

The odd couple had not grown apart; rather they'd become closer because of their different personalities.

The family reunion at Eaglehawk involved catching up on the news from Mornington. Tom and Jim were eager to know how Papa was going. And they delighted in hearing how the 'little ones' (Jack, Jeannie and Sallie) were growing up. Willie had the grim task of telling his brothers their favourite uncle Joe, who had lived as a farmer in Gippsland for many years, had died. Joe Caldwell was close to all his brother's children, particularly Willie. Jim, tugging his pipe thoughtfully, consoled Willie and said that when he returned to Victoria in 1892, after the harvest, he would go to Gippsland and fix up uncle Joe's farm, certain to be overrun by then.

'The animals will need care.'

Among Jim's new skills was his ability to break horses. He treated them with soft touches and whispering.

'Trust a horse for knowing a good master,' he liked to say after taming a wild one. 'There are plenty of horses that have a lot more sense than the people.'

His own horse, a chestnut named Mick, could buck him off at dawn but lie down for him in the stable at dusk. Mick's chief trick was to steal a handkerchief from Jim's pocket.

In Tasmania, Jim handled all the animals. When those on the farm became ill, he sat with them until they improved or died. When they died, and they usually did, he lit a smoke and went to choose another to take its place.

Between the practicalities of farm life, there was plenty of cheerfulness during Alice and Willie's visit. The Field cousins, aunties and uncles organised get-togethers. Willie seemed to like these events and others had fun with him. At a Sunday School picnic on the Westfield estate, the Caldwells' younger second cousins singled Willie out and 'got on to him' – as the kids had done at Frankston in the first game earlier that year. There was no apparent reason for this, except perhaps Willie looked easy to rile.

'Does your mother know you're out?' said one of the cousins.

'Yes,' Willie shot back. 'She gave me a penny and sent me to buy a brass monkey. Are you for sale?'

Willie's hazing continued at the picnic until he'd had enough and threw a tart at one of the loudmouth relatives. He missed and the pastry landed in a teacup being cradled by a rich aunty. By the time the splash hit the saucer, Willie was looking the other way.

Another day, the Field family invited the Caldwell brothers

to play tennis on a perfect lawn court, swept of leaves. Willie, not reading the upper-class script, turned up to play in an old coat and slouch hat, smoking a pipe. Jim told Alice about it later. 'You know what Bill is like when he is in one of his untidy moods,' he said. 'Like a ruffled bear.'

Alice was taken by how her cousins' children loved Jim, almost as much as the Caldwells' siblings back home. One memory stayed with her almost as long as she lived. A child was sick and could not stop crying. Jim visited after work and the girl went to him and sat on his knee, so comfortable she forgot she was upset. Another of the relatives, a boy, heard Jim was around and gave him a bunch of violets. He wanted to stick them through his second-uncle's buttonhole but the flowers wouldn't fit. Jim reached into his pocket for a penknife. Carefully enlarging the hole, he commented, memorably, 'Goodness me . . . the man [coat maker] must've been on the wine when he cut that.' The knife made a bigger hole and the violets went in. It made the boy's day.

Christmas came and went. The Caldwells savoured their time together and then parted. Alice and Willie travelled by ship back to Victoria. Before leaving, one of them asked Jim the time, noticing he still had his silver chain and locket, perhaps the only reminder now that, just over a year ago, this farmer had been a pale insurance man living a half-life back in Melbourne. Attached to his chain was Tom's watch, a gift from the eldest brother. It was time to go.

'See you after harvest,' Jim said to Alice and Willie. 'I promise.'

Twenty-two

Hugh toiled almost every day in the Allchin stable until the boat was remade. Charlie joined him on weekends. While shaping the hull, the teenagers (Charlie was still nineteen, turning twenty in May 1892) talked about their futures in a world that had no limits. All their plans involved being together, combining their trades of architecture and building. Inevitably, they discussed leaving Mornington and travelling further than Melbourne to other colonies and countries. London. California. Somewhere. Anywhere.

Hugh and Charlie were now as close as any friends. Those who knew them best could name the day their mateship first went this way. It was a Sunday morning during one of Willie's rare visits from Scotch; he had brought two pals from school home with him and they were planning a hunt. Rev. Caldwell was out of town on business and not coming back soon. The minister had left Hugh in charge of driving the replacement Presbyterian preacher around town.

Unsmiling for once, Hugh was preparing the buggy after breakfast. He knew a joyless day was at hand. He had to drive miles to pick up the clergyman and return him to Mornington for a late-morning service, then transport the minister to another town to perform in the afternoon. Willie and his friends were not waiting around. They began preparing their horses and guns.

Charlie came over. Instead of joining Willie, he went to Hugh.

'Heard you might need some help,' Charlie said. 'I'll come with you today if you like.'

Hugh was chuffed. He asked if he knew Willie and co. were heading into the bush. Charlie nodded. He had made his choice.

The boat rebuild took them longer than they had hoped.

Despite the Depression, Hugh's boss – J. D. Grover – was still busy finishing jobs that had been in the making for years. That meant Hugh was flat out, too. Main Street had expanded those past two years. Bricklayers, painters and other tradespeople were kept active enough. A coffee palace was being built beside the Cricketer's Arms Hotel.

Grover had won contracts to build the most important services to the town, namely gas lighting (Grover and his workers installed the lamps after the pipes were laid) and expansion of the pier and jetty.

For ten years visiting politicians had been asked to 'make the jetty longer' so the steamers could dock more easily. But it had been costed at six thousand pounds. By now the original breakwater, built in the 1850s, was aging.

Eventually the money came. Pile driving went ahead, before the decking was laid to make the jetty 100 feet longer. On big worksites like that, tradesmen barely notice apprentices but Hugh, as usual, made an impression.

One particularly sweaty day, one of J. D. Grover's senior carpenters dropped his expensive new hammer into deep water; he swore and stood aghast. He told his colleagues he couldn't swim. Hugh said he would go in and fetch it. 'If you get me a pair of old pants . . . I'll get your hammer for you,' he said.

There were fishermen nearby, sorting nets beside boats. They could help find a spare pair of trousers, no worries. Hugh went to one of the old storage sheds on the sand and changed. On his return to the pier, the aggrieved builder pointed to the splash spot.

Hugh dived in and disappeared, resurfacing twice with a frustrated look and no tool. His swimming strength was on display now. Few men could have dived once let alone three times. All witnesses admired him and probably wondered how such a big lad (weighing about twelve stone) could float so well.

'Good going, Hughie,' someone encouraged.

His third try was successful. He came up smiling. The builder was so grateful he offered Hugh money.

'Oh no, I couldn't think of such a thing,' Hugh said, and waved away a shilling being handed to him.

'Then come up to one of the hotels with me and have a drink,' said the builder.

Hughie said it wasn't necessary. He later told his family back at the manse, 'I was only too glad to get the man his hammer. Poor fellow.'

Away from his busy working hours, Hugh finally reconstructed his first seaworthy vessel. Charlie was just as eager to try it out on Port Phillip. The sheepish owners launched it once more, this time with less fanfare. The boat floated and within minutes Hugh and Charlie knew the flat bottom was a better design. It sailed just fine and for the rest of the summer they would be seen touring the edges of the bay, fishing or just enjoying a ride.

Charlie, who had suffered from seasickness as a child, reported in a letter to his brother in Queensland that he was cured.

On the few Sundays the pair went hunting instead of fishing they left their runabout on the sand. A problem arose when they found out some children were taking the new boat for joy rides. One day Hugh and Charlie went to use it, only to see it floating away, skippered by two or three kids aged between ten and fifteen. 'Bloomin' youngsters,' said Hugh, who was only a few years older. It was more embarrassing than he thought; the children had rigged a makeshift sail from their clothes and were cruising naked. Unable to properly navigate by 'shirt sail', the thieves spent an entire afternoon out to sea, eventually washing up on some rocks beneath the cliffs north of The Point. The kids fled and were lucky to escape injury, but must have had a scare.

'Serves them right, too,' Charlie was heard to say.

Hugh and Charlie decided not to let this happen again. The next week they watched their boat on the sand from a secret spot among the ti-trees to see if the 'mischievous imps' would come back. They did. Hugh and Charlie then issued justice by dunking the children's heads in the shallows. Onlookers heard the children pleading, 'Oh, Hughie, I will never do it again . . . Hughie, it wasn't me.'

Hugh and Charlie decided the 'boat was everybody's but their own' and that it'd be better to anchor it in the harbour. Hugh found a big rock, took it to a workshop in Main Street and had inserted into it an iron ring, attaching a chain long enough to go from the boat to the weight, with enough slack to cope with tidal changes. The pair rowed to a distance far enough away from the pier and jetty. Hugh dropped the rock over the side, making sure he kept possession of one end of the chain.

The scheme's chief problem was obvious to all. Every time they wanted to take the boat out they had to undress on the beach and swim for it. When they reached the boat they had to throw the chain over the edge, paddle in for their clothes and, now dressed, sail away. On returning they would have to go to the beach, strip, paddle out and find the anchor. Then came the toughest test: diving for the rock's ring to feed through the chain. Hugh dived more often but Charlie could swim well and this shared chore made him even stronger.

Often it was dark when they were diving for the rock. The bay was cold, even in early summer, and a fast immersion was enough to steal a swimmer's breath, holding it ransom for a few seconds before giving it back. Hugh and Charlie learned you could not escape the shock of the cold, but it would pass within a minute or two. Fear of sharks was the last challenge they had to conquer.

The Caldwell family was sitting in the breakfast room one evening when Hugh came home wet.

'Hughie,' his sister Alice said, 'what on earth have you been doing? Not bathing at this time of night, surely?'

Hugh explained he had been for a 'row' after tea. 'Poor old Charlie,' he said. 'He didn't like going into the water at all. He stood on the side of the boat and looked at the water and said, "It does look cold, and there may be sharks about." But I said, "Charlie, come on," and dived in, and he after me, and we came ashore in a brace of the shakes.'

One day Sarah Allchin asked her son about his boat.

'Charlie, whatever would you boys do if anything went wrong . . . when you are out on the bay?'

Charlie smiled so his mother would see there was nothing to be concerned about.

'Hughie and I are like corks in the water,' he said. 'We would just swim round and put her [the boat] right, and get in again.'

Sarah left it there, perhaps wondering what would happen if they could not put her right.

Twenty-three

It was early autumn in 1892 when Jim and Tom Caldwell stood upon the railway platform at Westbury in Tasmania. They were listening for the whistle, peering at the tree line for the approaching steam. Jim had his bags by his side. The season's heavy work was over and he was going back to Victoria. Tom was staying behind to take care of Eaglehawk. The train arrived. The brothers shook hands: one clean grip, a single shake, and a hold. They looked at each other's eyes as Papa had always taught them. Tom used to say to others that he had never met anyone who could look you more fair in the face than Jim.

It was not clear to either of them why they were so moved by this farewell. Tom was particularly emotional. He was proud of his little brother's transformation. Jim had arrived in Tasmania the picture of ill health. Now look at him.

Growing up, Jim had been the cheeky one. Once, in

Mr Worrell's Mornington State School class, the teacher started the day by admonishing late-arriving pupils.

'It is well for everybody to be early,' said Mr Worrell. 'It is the early bird that catches the worm.'

'It is not very well for the worm, sir,' said Jim, grinning.

Tom loved that Jim's youthful spark had returned.

Now he was sad to see his brother leaving and something made him say, without any reason he could discover then or when he laboured on it later, 'Shall we ever meet again?'

Jim said he would return by winter. Then the train came and took him and the brothers waved goodbye.

Twenty-four

The autumn Mornington people would never forget was rain soaked, just like the one before it. The town looked as handsome as ever. But the people were anxious about floods, disease and the Depression. The talk on Main Street was that the whole place was in a 'state of sop'.

The excursion steamers had stopped coming in April. Holiday season was done. No more picnics with merry-go-round games, Punch and Judy shows and singing under the trees. It had not been a memorable summer. The locals had done everything possible to spin the tourist pound. Back in October the shire had hired painters to give a fresh coat to the post office and other shire buildings. Residents were urged by noticeboard to do the same while waiting for the ships to arrive . . .

Port Phillip steamers had been running people, stores and mail across and around the bay since 1854. By the 1870s Melburnians were keen to pay for excursions down the coast. Paddle steamers were fitted with restaurants and full-time musical bands.

In the booming 1880s faster steamers were imported and more people – sometimes up to a thousand a day – took weekend trips to Mornington. With fishing stocks dwindling from the overuse of nets, tourism had become The Point's biggest earner. But the steamer season of 1891/92 had been lousy. Hoteliers and boarding-house operators bemoaned a 'dullness of trade'.

A series of deaths added to the sadness in Mornington and surrounding towns during this time. A fruit farmer called George James was found dead in his property. One end of a length of string was attached to the trigger of his rifle, the other end tied to his boot. The back of his skull had been blown away. The first police officer on the scene later said the self-inflicted death was a 'most determined one'.

Suicide was becoming more common, due to the failing economy. Storeowners, like the Allchins, knew people were really struggling when customers started buying bread by the slice and candles by halves. Increasingly, wealthier locals began getting 'calls' from desperate townsfolk 'pleading distress and want of employment'. Begging was illegal and people had been prosecuted for it. In one case, Rev. Caldwell was called to give evidence for the prosecution after it was revealed he had given a man with 'no lawful visible means of support' some food. The minister was described in documents as 'an unwilling witness'.

Yet another death made headlines after a body was found lying on the side of the road between Mornington and Frankston. Locals knew the deceased as 'Black Aleck', a local

Indigenous man. His real name was Aleck Tyson. He was twenty-four and had worked in the area as a labourer since he was a boy.

Locals reckoned Black Aleck was drunk riding his horse and had fallen off. One of the stirrups was found near the body. The dead man was carried to the Tanti Hotel and an inquest was held. The whispers were true. Aleck had been drinking before his accident. Who had sold him booze? Publicans knew, or should have known, that the local law forbade them selling liquor to 'aboriginal people'.

A month later Senior Constable Murphy brought charges against the owners of the Cricketers Arms in Main Street and the Tanti Hotel, where the inquest was held. Witnesses told the Mornington Police Court they saw 'the black served with drink in the hotels mentioned'. A lawyer for the publicans said the Cricketers Arms owner thought Aleck was 'an Indian'. The bench said ignorance was no excuse and fined each of the defendants five pounds.

Not all seaside dramas had ended in tragedy. Panic seized the local crowd at Mornington baths one summer day when a young woman, who could not swim, staggered into water above her head. The owner, Councillor William Irvine, sprang from his office and dived fully clothed into the bay to find the woman's submerged body. His actions were so fast the lady was conscious while being dragged into the shore. Cr Irvine was celebrated for his gallantry.

Brave acts became contagious. Late in the holiday season, the steamer *Ozone* almost crushed a man to death against the pier. A strong wind was blowing from the west, making it difficult for the ferry to pull aside the jetty. The gangway was extended but barely touched the *Ozone*. A man named Fred Coppin, a well-known visitor from Sorrento, was standing nearby and he tried to secure the gangway but overbalanced and fell in the water between the jetty and ship. The *Ozone*'s captain showed composure to steady his vessel while ordering Mr Coppin to be hauled out. It all happened within a few heartbeats and the Sorrento man survived his dunking.

Then the rain came and stayed for weeks.

Twenty-five

In 1892, the Queen's Birthday long weekend was scheduled to begin on Saturday, 21 May. Two Mornington families were particularly excited by the promise of a four-day holiday: the Allchins couldn't wait for Charlie to come home for a longer than usual spell; and the Caldwells were hopeful both Jim and Willie would make it back to the manse by Friday. Rev. Caldwell was so excited that seven of his eight children might be under the one roof he ordered a fattened calf to be slaughtered.

Jim was still in Gippsland, on the other side of Western Port bay, a two-day ride from Mornington. After arriving home from Tasmania, he had spent six weeks back at The Point before going to care for his late uncle Joe's abandoned property. In letters to Papa he had explained that uncle Joe's house was too damp to live in, so he had been sleeping in the spare room at a neighbour's place. The neighbour didn't have much bread in the house so Jim went hungry on the first night and had to be satisfied with smoking pipe after pipe. In other letters Jim explained his work on uncle Joe's farm included repairing fences, clearing the land, taking care of the animals. The rain had been so bad he could not cross the swollen river to go to town and buy meat, so he was reduced to shooting and eating wallabies.

'The wallaby is a nice change from the ordinary butcher's meat,' he wrote.

Twenty-six

By the afternoon of Tuesday 17 May, Jim had finished his work; he was determined to make it back to The Point by the weekend. Torrential rain had stopped him from leaving Joe's the previous day. Next morning he had decided to go – no matter what. Now he was riding his horse, Mick, and leading another, a filly he'd all but tamed in his late uncle's paddock. Jim was saturated but happy to be on one of the old Boon Wurrung trails going west on a journey he guessed was fifty or sixty miles.

The drenched bush was old country, a part of the peninsula that had not been cleared by loggers and replanted with English trees to remind his parents' generation of home. Jim knew this land well because he had hunted here with his brothers. Throughout the 1880s, Easter and Christmas holidays were for camping. When Mornington filled with visitors the boys spilled out, to go on a peaceful exploration of the hills, valleys and headlands of Australia's rugged southern coastline. Charlie Allchin was with the Caldwells on most of these trips.

They usually set off from their homes at night to avoid the heat. As the colours of dusk crept across the horizon, Charlie would say farewell to his parents, scoring a plum cake and a kiss from Sarah, and swing by the Caldwell stables. Boots and guns cleaned, the party would then head out to find a track, destination not that important, just away. Up to twenty miles would be covered by first sun-up. Usually they went all the way to the bottom of the mainland, past the limestone Cape Schanck lighthouse, built in the 1850s to oversee the ocean.

The boys carried canvas tents but also looked for abandoned huts or even farmhouses, somewhere to make a fire, rest and feed the horses, while a tree branch and two forked sticks held the billy on the boil. Food came from straight shooting or the saddlebags, which always carried tinned grub and Charlie's mum's plum cake. The Caldwells also had a plum pudding but would save it until it was really needed. Once the travellers ate corned beef bought from a bush store. It didn't kill them but it made them sick and gave them something to grimace and laugh about later.

Other sources of amusement were the residents they met on their longest rides. A woman they knew in Gippsland always made them smile. They called her 'Mother Battleaxe' – sharp-tongued Jim was the most likely to have named her – because of her 'hardness of character'.

Apparently, the Caldwell brothers did not write about these trips in diaries, or at least none of their writings remain. But Charlie Allchin liked to tell his brother in Queensland about his adventures through letters. The following is an extract from a letter Charlie wrote in 1887. He was fifteen and had just enjoyed a fun but painful day of fishing on the bay with Hugh Caldwell and J. D. Grover.

> Please excuse the writing as a flathead ran a prick in my thumb. We had wonderful luck, he caught 3 and I caught 3, the boat was drifting at such a rate the sinkers would not keep the bottom [sic]. The afternoon before New Year's Day we went out with a fisherman for about an hour and a half . . . We caught a basket of flatheads . . . The flathead reefs are all shifting now so you can't catch many.

Then he told about hunting with the Caldwells.

> I have knocked 4 hares so far. We went out . . . walked about 70 miles . . . I got up at half past three and woke all the others. We got 8 hares in [a farmer's] paddock . . . Altogether we got 14 hares, 1 kangaroo, 1 rabbit.

He explained that a man named Banks had joined their party while they were shooting closer to Mornington.

> Mr Banks blew a snakes head off that was going for one of his dogs and he blew a hare very nearly in half that ran too close to him. Only its backbone was left. Bill Caldwell shot the kangaroo in the throat. We saw 10 and we are the only ones on the Point that know where they are.

Then Charlie wrote about Jim.

> Jim Caldwell and I went out after dinner one day. It is only 8 miles . . . Jim planted [his feet] at the log fence and I went round and came down through the paddock and banged my gun off.
>
> A flying doe and a joey came past Jim. He rolled the old one over on the road but it got up and cleared with two dogs on it. They pulled it down and came back with blood all over them. When we went to look for it we started another flyer but the dogs never saw it and we had left our guns on the road. We never got either.

Perhaps Jim was thinking about these hunting adventures while he tied the horses up and said something kind to them, unfurled his tent, swung it over a frame of sticks and yanked them tight to the ground with some rope. Maybe he was flush with those memories as he smoked his pipe and listened to the wildlife. Or maybe, like any young man, he wasn't contemplating the past at all. More likely he was thinking about tomorrow. Wednesday. He would soon be home with his family.

Twenty-seven

Next afternoon, Mornington and its surrounding hills were in low cloud. A slight wind ruffled trees and bushes. Smoke rose from every fireplace. The Caldwells' blazes were well made in several rooms. Rev. Caldwell was away on a church errand. His age – sixty-seven – was not slowing him; the minister continued to tour the peninsula and even became involved in events at other churches. The Wesleyan Church had not long ago celebrated an anniversary with a ceremony of songs, duets, readings and recitations. The Allchin family was pleased to see Rev. Caldwell there. The local press noted:

> In this 'Queen of Watering Places' it may be said that bigotry and narrowness have no place and as the Rev. Mr Caldwell put, 'the churches esteem one another in love'.

When he wasn't serving the community he was meeting with district leaders in different guises. He still held an important seat on a five-man committee called a Board of Advice. This was a government-appointed gathering of three councillors and two gentlemen – Rev. Caldwell was the board's community 'correspondent' – to map strategic planning for the district. He was also marrying people all over the place, as he had done for more than three decades, the most recent a couple in the Western Port town of Somerville. He was famous for giving 'solemn' weddings.

So the mobile minister was not home to hear the footsteps on the veranda. Alice and the three little ones were in the breakfast room. The eldest was reading about the serial murderer Alfred Deeming in the *Argus*. Deeming had killed his wife and children in England and another woman in Melbourne; he had been sentenced to hang the following week. Alice was reading so intently she did not hear the clomping on the porch until it became louder and moved toward the front door. Who is it? she wondered. It couldn't be Willie. He was still in Melbourne. Hughie was at work and never came home early from Mr Grover's. Could it be Jim?

'It must be . . .' she said. 'Jim?'

The smaller children were thrilled just at the chance it might be him. Their memories of his coming home at weekends when he lived in East Melbourne were sweet. Each Saturday he would arrive at the front gate, where Jack, Sallie and Jeannie would be waiting, to tell him about the new animals born or what was in the kitchen for dinner. But they wouldn't look him in the eye for long. His pockets were more interesting to anyone under ten because they always carried lollies.

'What did you bring?' one would say reaching in.

'Hold on, hold on,' Jim would order. 'One at a time.'

Jim would give Jack his overnight bag, if it wasn't too heavy. He would hold onto the treats for a few more minutes, enjoying the anticipation on his siblings' faces. 'When we get up to the house.'

Only once were the children disappointed, when Jim brought them 'coconut ice'. Alice had to trade it for her chocolate to make them happy again. That was about three years ago.

The sound of the boots didn't stop at the front door. Alice was still perplexed. It can't be Jim, she thought. It was too wet outside. There was no way he would have ridden from Gippsland in this weather.

'Hughie, is that you?' she called out.

There was silence from the visitor.

'Jim, is that you?' she called.

Alice placed her newspaper down and went into the hall. There was Jim in his dripping macintosh and leggings. He was mud-covered. His boots were leaking brown rain.

'My darling,' said Alice, hugging him. 'Why didn't you answer me?'

Jack, Sallie and Jeannie enveloped him and squealed from becoming wet and dirty at once.

Alice told him to dry off and replace his clothes. She warned he might catch a cold.

'No fear,' Jim said. 'I have got along with them for the best part of two days, and now I guess they will stay on for a little while longer.'

They walked into the breakfast room and Jim edged as close as possible to the fireplace. The little ones huddled near.

'Something like a fire,' Jim said, trying to figure how long it had been since he saw one as impressive. He told Alice all his fires had been 'miserable' at uncle Joe's house.

'I thought that bush people were famous for fires,' Alice teased.

'They ought to be,' he said.

Alice boiled some water to use for tea. She and her brother talked about his time in Gippsland. He explained how much work he had done to improve the property. Alice thought he looked as well as ever. After some food, he went to check on his horses: Mick and the filly.

The sky had brightened. Locals started coming out of their homes, as if some battle had now ceased and it was finally safe.

Alice, wearing a coat and scarf, joined Jim in the stables. He boasted how he had broken in the young horse. Alice was still nervous around the animals.

'Look,' she said. 'She's going to kick. Look, Jim, she is laying back her ears.'

'If she did,' Jim said, 'I would give her such a whacking she would not do it again in a hurry, I warrant.' Instead, he caressed the horse. Alice did the same.

A voice called out to them. It was old Archibald Cook, their neighbour. He was now approaching across the Caldwells' yard.

'Glad to see you back home again,' Mr Cook said. Jim said thank you.

'When will you be in?' asked Mr Cook, meaning when would Jim come over to his house for a cigar and talk.

'Not tonight,' Jim said. 'But tomorrow night, how will that suit you?'

'Fine,' said Mr Cook. 'I have a friend that always comes up for a game of cards on a Thursday evening.'

The friendly neighbour left Alice and Jim alone. Alice again urged her brother to go and take off his damp clothes. She told him he would be sick if he didn't. But Jim was resilient and he would not fall ill. Alice was the one who would catch a cold.

So began a series of small events that would reshape their family for all time. In fact, every decision and every moment from now until Saturday would determine the growth of family trees all over the peninsula.

Twenty-eight

After work on Thursday, Mornington's footballers gathered at their home ground, where the grass was no longer puddled, to practise before their next game of the season. At the start of training the team was talking about hosting a strong opponent from the town of Mordialloc.

The Mordialloc club had placed a note in the newspaper promoting the fixture, along with its team list, which included journeymen Droop and Millman. With a grin, Hugh told his teammate that his brother Jim was in town and might be convinced to play on the weekend.

'What about Willie?' someone said.

'I'm not sure if he'll be back,' replied Hugh, who only knew 'Old Bill' was going to watch the big rowing race on the Yarra the next day. 'He might rush home if he knows Jim has arrived.'

The possibility of having three Caldwell brothers in the one team for the very first time excited the whole club.

Hugh also confirmed his best mate would be playing; Charlie had taken part in the first two games of the season, a scratch match and a win over the Rovers, which had decided at a general meeting to 're-establish the club'.

The football team was now in its fifth season (counting those few games in 1887 before the club's formation in 1888) and change was evident. The older sportsmen in the district were slowing as the game quickened. Though scrimmages still marred wet matches, the dash and swerve of ball runners were on the rise. Passing had also become more precise. Youngsters, who had been raised on the game and could therefore best judge the flight and bounce of an oval ball, were bringing a higher level of skill to the senior ranks.

The new faces at Mornington's practice session were smooth and fresh. The club had unearthed some teenagers who would see them through a full schedule. Mature men in their thirties were still playing cricket but were unlikely to keep lining up for the winter struggle.

One of the first-year players was seventeen-year-old John Kinna (always misspelled as Kenna on the team sheet). He was a local telegraph operator. His parents, bootmaker James and wife Emily, from free-settling families, had married at Tarradale in Gippsland; they had three children, including John, their eldest.

When the cricket team came together in November the previous year, Kinna was a surprise selection. No one had known the lad could bowl so well. In one match, he took eight wickets. It was hoped he could kick goals as prolifically.

Three days before the cricket season ended, annual general football meetings were scheduled.

The first was held to decide whether the Rovers should go on as they had in their first breakaway season. The last match the Rovers had played in 1891 was against Dromana and such was the crossover of players from the Mornington original team that Dromana's committee complained:

> Dromana followers were shocked but maybe not surprised to see many of the Rovers were from the 'Mornington First Twenty'.

With so many players changing teams, were the Rovers needed? The answer might be found in the census for the County of Mornington. A few months before the 1892 season, the Mornington shire had expanded to house almost 4000 people in 755 homes. Simply, it could be argued Mornington was big enough for two teams, no matter how they were selected.

The *Standard* reported without analysis:

> It was decided to re-establish the club, known last year as the Rovers Football Club.

Money from last year was tallied and a membership subscription set at just over two shillings. Officials were elected. The new Rovers president was shire councillor Alfred Downward, who at that time was running for state parliament.

Downward wanted people to know he was one of them so he went to all public gatherings he could, including football meetings. By the end of the month he would be president of at least three peninsula clubs.

Five days later the Mornington Football Club held its general meeting. A committee was elected and a rough fixture drawn up. Mornington's first match would be against the Rovers on 7 May.

There was no bitterness in Main Street conversations in the weeks leading to the local derby. Some families might have taken it more seriously than others, but the class divide had been backfilled by a season of mutual respect.

Of the Caldwells, only Hugh was to play. Jim was in Gippsland and Willie in Melbourne with no promise of returning for the weekend. Charlie arrived back from Melbourne in time for the game. There were several other very young players on the team, including William Grover, son of J. D. Grover, whose brother (also William) was also to line up. Another interesting inclusion was John Kinna, notwithstanding his father was on the Rovers Football Club committee. It summed up the looseness of selection in the two-team town.

The match report was succinct and respectful to both teams, although probably penned by a member of the Mornington club.

> These rival clubs met for the first time this season on Saturday last (7th) on the ground of the former. Great interest was taken in the game and there was a numerous attendance of the supporters of the respective teams. The day was fine and the ground in splendid playing order and a fast game was anticipated. When play commenced, it was soon seen that the senior

team were in the better trim, and they had their opponents at their mercy all through the game, kicking five goals and nine behinds to one goal and four behinds.

Charlie Allchin didn't get a mention. But Hugh, as usual, had scored. Willie Coles was noted as first man in the best players list. Short, who played close to goals every game, slotted a pair of goals. It was significant that Tom Coxhell was an important player. His name was being mentioned as a possible full-time captain. A man named William Bennett was the only one injured in the game. The father-of-four broke his collarbone and would not play again that year.

So the season began in a flurry of matches across the district and all the way down the peninsula. Right up until the Thursday evening training session before the Mordialloc match, Mornington's men believed they were to next play a home game. But then a suggestion came for a change of venue. It might have come as the players stood on the side of the field regaining their breath after training, though more likely it came an hour later as the team lounged in the front room of Kirkpatrick's Hotel overlooking the lightless Port Phillip. The idea belonged to fisherman Charles Hooper. From beneath his thick moustache came the words, 'We could sail to the match.'

He offered his boat the *Process* as transport.

'I'll put on her racing sails,' he said, promising there would be a 'fair wind'.

Not everyone was thrilled by his proposition. But some were. A debate followed. There are no minutes of this meeting so it wasn't an official club discussion. Rather it was a bunch of blokes working out what they might want to do with their Saturday. Later it was said that a dozen of the players wanted to 'go by sea'. It is easy to believe a majority of those present put their hands up when the vote came to take the *Process*. Most of those were younger players. They had nothing to lose, nothing to fear. Getting home in the dark? Don't even think about it. Let's just play the game and worry about that later.

Jim Caldwell was not at Kirkpatrick's and although Hugh had mentioned that his older brother might play against Mordialloc, there was little chance. Jim had spent the afternoon drying out and caring for his horses. At the same time the team was training, Jim was dressing in warm clothes to fulfil his promise to the Caldwells' nearest neighbour, Mr Cook. He assumed they would play cards and smoke cigars. A pipe was already in his hand.

Jim asked Alice if she wanted to come but his sister said she wasn't feeling well. She sounded congested when she explained she didn't want to breathe the dreaded night air.

'Can't you wrap up?' Jim asked between puffs.

'Well, even if I did, I would get my feet wet, after all this rain.'

'No, you needn't,' Jim said. He offered to carry her.

'Oh, Jim, what a nonsense.' Alice said.

'No nonsense about it at all.'

'But Jim, really, it would be madness for me to go out tonight,' Alice said.

'Very well,' said Jim. And off he went, leaving his sister to have a much-needed early night.

Twenty-nine

On Friday, Hugh woke at dawn and dressed for work, hoeing into some bread and butter before leaving the quiet house. Birds were nattering outside, enjoying the second rainless sky in a row. A thin spread of dew made the grass sparkle. The air was crisp.

Hugh had assumed Jim was still asleep but the elder brother had bounced out of bed earlier and was now tending his horses in the stables.

'Did you hear the news?' Hugh asked.

Jim shook his head and Hugh explained how the football match against Mordialloc would be changed to an away game. And they were going to sail to it. He explained there was still uncertainty about player numbers. Worse case, the team could field one or two short, or recruit barrackers. Mordialloc might even lend a player, if needed, though Droop and Millman wouldn't be allowed to change colours again.

Jim disappointed Hugh by showing little interest but said he'd think about it. Instead he seemed in deep thought about something else, maybe Tom and Eaglehawk. He had been away for such a long time.

The brothers discussed in a few short sentences whether Willie would be coming home that weekend and concluded no one could know for sure. Hugh said goodbye to Jim and flashed across the yard via the fruit trees, pocketing a few for mid-morning snacks. Then he went to J. D. Grover's workshop.

Hugh loved his job and never dawdled to work. The business was on the corner of Main and Barkly streets and was always full of workers, customers or friends. Often it felt like a family home because the boss' children came to play before and after school. Forty-one-year-old J. D. Grover was married with five children. His wife, Ellen, was pregnant with number six, due in November.

At seventeen, Hugh was the same age as his employer's eldest son William, who had left the family business to work as an accountant at the Commercial Bank for star football goal sneak Henry Short. Hugh and William were top mates.

Another William Grover, J. D.'s much younger brother, was a builder at the workshop. The twenty-six-year-old was married with one child. He was fit enough to still play football and was looking forward to the trip to Mordialloc. So the two Grover representatives on the team the next day would both be named William: uncle and nephew.

Since he was first apprenticed, Hugh had helped watch over most of the younger Grover siblings before and after school at the timber yard. One day, little Edgar Grover was skylarking near a stack of timber when he tripped and fell, the wood toppling upon him. Hugh saw it but couldn't stop it. He lifted the timber up and made sure the lad was okay before sending the injured Grover to see his mother. Acting the adult, he then said to a colleague, 'Serve the young beggar right, he had been told over and over not to go near the timber in case of it falling on him.'

Alice later recalled in her book *Love's Tribute*:

> Another day I was passing Mr Grover's place of business, and seeing Hughie in the yard, I watched him without him noticing me. He had just brought something down from the workshop, which he placed in the conveyance where Mr Grover was already seated. Seeing that the children were going to accompany their father, he lifted the little fellows in one by one, and stood watching them as they all drove off with an amused smile on his handsome face at the little boys' pleasure.

J. D. Grover was not only an esteemed builder and sportsman, he was also a talented singer, winning loud cheers at concerts. Locals remembered for a long time the way he sang at a state school fundraiser in 1889, an event chaired by Rev. Caldwell.

The *South Bourke and Mornington Journal* noted on May 22 1889:

> Mr. J. D. Grover's rendering of 'The owl' and 'I seek for thee in every flower' had a very pleasing effect upon the audience, being sung in a sweet and tasteful manner, and the singer was accorded a well merited round of applause.

J. D. then sang a duet with the school principal Mr Walker, as Charlie Allchin's sister Ella played the piano. The press review read:

> This, in my opinion and without wishing to detract from the others their due need of praise, was the vocal gem of the evening, the rendering of which elicited rounds of applause.

Their song was *Old Albion*. One of J. D.'s other favourite songs was *My Pretty Jane*.

> My pretty Jane! my pretty Jane!
> Ah! never, never look so shy.
> But meet me, meet me in the Ev'ning,
> While the bloom is on the Rye.

And if he wanted to whistle the tune in the workshop no one would have complained, least of all apprentice Hugh, particularly on Fridays while daydreaming about sailing and playing football the next day.

Thirty

As Hugh worked at the top end of Main Street, there was much excitement at the harbour below. Fishermen, who had been out catching flathead all morning, were sorting their baskets, sharing the news that a famous yacht would arrive the next day. All had heard of the imminent arrival of the *Wanderer* and its famous skipper H. P. Fergie, a leading Melbourne businessman and around-the-world adventurer. Apparently he was bringing with him some other well-known sailors, including the outstanding bay racer Arthur Peck. Promise of such celebrities at The Point gave the locals a thrill.

Already down at the water's edge was Charles Hooper, preparing his *Process* for the football trip of a lifetime. Never before had a team from Mornington sailed to a match. It was rare enough for the club to play away games. Most opponents preferred to come to The Point. But the arrangements had been made by now. Mordialloc had agreed to prepare its field and Hooper was charged with taking his teammates fifteen miles up the coast.

Charles Hooper was a thirty-four-year-old burly fisherman and a father of four. He hailed from Geelong, where he married a local woman, Maria Gowty, in 1877. Charles and Maria had four children: their youngest was a newborn named Ernest; their eldest was Charles Frederick Hooper, who at thirteen years was his father's deckhand apprentice. Hooper had relocated from Geelong to Mornington to fish the bay from the east. Western Port was the best spot for commercial fishing in 1892 but Mornington was just across Port Phillip from Geelong, where Maria still lived with her extended family. Charles was always going back and forth.

Hooper and the *Process* were well regarded in Mornington. Not only was he a successful fisherman, he was a well-performed yachtsman in local regattas. After the first Mornington regatta was held at Easter in 1887 – to celebrate the Queen's Jubilee – it had become an annual event. Within a year it began attracting entrants from around the bay. Hooper's finest year was 1891, when he triumphed over five others from Melbourne and Frankston.

The *Process* would be described today as a couta boat, even though the term wasn't used for it then. The model was made to survive the several hundred miles of deadly Bass Strait and Great Southern Ocean coastline between fishing towns in Victoria from Portland in the far west to Port Albert in Gippsland. The name 'couta' came later because a lot of crews, although not all, were chasing barracouta to sell to fish-and-chip shops.

These boats were not all crafted alike. They varied in length, depth and rigging. The *Process* was a type most common to Port Phillip. It was big enough to carry large nets but light enough to steer easily and beach without breaking. It had a double-ended centreboard (retractable keel) that could be removed in shallow water or while the nets were being hauled in. Hooper ran the *Process* with 'lug sails' (two mainsails flown from an Oregon mast and a yard, which moved up and down the mast to raise the sails). A wire 'halyard' was used to lift the mainsail yard up the foremast. The halyard was attached to the deck at the other end. The boat also had a small 'mizzen-mast' at the rear.

Some of these boats were so fast and manoeuvrable they began being entered in races. Regattas were held throughout Port Phillip and along the west coast of Victoria. Few had a better read of the wind than those who drifted with it every day of their working lives. So people like Hooper volunteered to test their skills against all comers. And to make his boat go faster, Hooper bought new sails reserved specifically for competition.

The regattas usually had six events: 'yachts exceeding 10 tons', 'yachts not exceeding 10 tons', 'trading vessels not exceeding 40 tons', 'centre plate yachts exceeding 23ft', 'centre plate yachts not exceeding 23ft', and 'centre plate sailing boats belonging to bona fide fishermen'.

The latter event was Hooper's to win.

Lining up at Mornington on a rare fine day in autumn 1891, Hooper had waited his turn as timekeeper J. D. Grover staggered the start according to handicap. The *Process* was one of seven entrants.

A gentleman from the Royal Yacht Club of Victoria came from Melbourne to sanction the regatta and act as judge.

Hundreds barracked for Hooper and shouted out whenever the *Process* came near enough that the skipper might hear voices from the cliffs. The wind was light – a yachting expert called the day's sport 'little more than a series of drifting matches owing to the lack of wind' – and sailors struggled for any speed. Eventually the judge declared the original distance of twenty-four miles (twice around a twelve-mile course) should be shortened to eighteen miles. It still took Hooper almost five hours to finish but he came in first, a few minutes before the runner-up.

Hooper won races in Mornington and Frankston and placed third in Geelong, but closer examination of his performances can reveal more about this competitor. The Monday before his winning Mornington race, Hooper had entered into the Frankston regatta. The weather was so bleak organisers thought they might have to postpone the whole event.

The *Standard* wrote about it this way:

> Heavy squally weather broke upon the morning of the Frankston Regatta, and the result was much to be deplored, as the committee had evidently gone to some amount of exertion. It was no fault of theirs that the meeting was not a success. Many of the boats which had competed at Schnapper Point failed to make the passage to Frankston, and were forced to put back, whilst other intending competitors remained at their moorings at Mordialloc and other points.

By early afternoon the sky appeared less menacing and the races were called on, though rain continued to fall as mist. Twenty-eight entrants across all races were reduced to twelve. The 'weather bound' non-starters did not include the

Process. Hooper wanted to race regardless of the conditions. He turned up to compete against three other boats: *Seagull*, *Petrel* and *Spray*.

Seagull finished the race twenty minutes before *Petrel*. Both boats were skippered by Frankston fishermen so the umbrella-sheltered spectators were happy they'd braved the day. Hooper had an awful time during the race and did not finish the course. The *Leader*, a weekly Melbourne newspaper, had sent its yachting correspondent 'Spinnaker' to cover the regatta. Spinnaker wrote of Hooper:

> Process (Mornington) carried away her mast in coming to the regatta, and was in difficulties several times during the race in consequence. She did not complete the course.

This incident raises questions about Hooper, for good or ill. Did his decision to press on despite weather and equipment problems make him a captain of unusual determination or suggest he could be reckless? Did the *Process* have an ongoing problem with her mast or did she simply struggle when the bay was not calm?

'Spinnaker' wrote in his summary of all races at Frankston that it was 'spoilt by a succession of squalls'. Squalls crossing Port Phillip in daylight come from the west and can be anticipated by experienced fishermen. They come with low cloud, rain and extra chop. Hooper could have prepared for them in the way he handled his sails. He would have dealt with these conditions often at work. Were the squalls too much for his wire halyard, which held the mast and sails in place?

What if Hooper didn't see a squall coming?

Perhaps these questions were asked at the time. More likely they weren't. Four days later, in breathless conditions at Mornington, he won the fishermen's race. Few in the crowd that fine day would have travelled to see his Frankston debacle. They would only have read about him being 'in difficulties several times'.

Hooper had no chance of redeeming himself at the next Frankston regatta. The 1892 event was ruined completely by rain. Organisers held out as long as they could but called it off and eventually postponed it until Boxing Day. They thought about running it on the Queen's Birthday weekend but by then it would be colder, and the football season would have taken over. The Mornington regatta did not go ahead in 1892. No reason was given in the press reports. The *Standard* published this in April.

> Very general surprise is expressed that no effort was made for holding the usual Mornington regatta on Easter Saturday. It had been pointed out that in previous years every regatta has been a success and it has been looked upon by yachtsmen to be an established institution. It is therefore hoped that efforts will be made next year for holding the annual regatta.

It is probable the Depression that had diminished numbers arriving for picnics aboard the bay steamers had also dimmed the enthusiasm for water sports.

But now Hooper had a chance to use his racing sails after all. On the Friday before taking the team out, he had several visitors, who stood on the jetty to talk to him. They saw he had help from his son Charles Frederick Hooper and another fisherman,

John Coomber, a friend from Geelong. Coomber was a thirty-one-year-old married father of four. His eldest was ten and his youngest three. His family was still in his hometown across the other side of the bay. Though few in town knew Coomber, he was a fit bloke and could play football well enough. Hooper had volunteered his services for the game against Mordialloc.

The *Process* looked in top shape, painted white with a gold streak. Hooper was removing her nets and had laid out her lug sails. The vessel – twenty-eight feet long, two feet eight inches deep – was five years old, a product of a boat builder named Hansen in Williamstown. Its centreboard could dip six feet under. His 'regatta' sails were going on the foremast. A 'working' sail would stay on the mizzenmast.

Senior Constable Thomas Murphy, the football club vice-president as well as general caretaker of the town's safety, stopped by to see if Hooper was serious about taking so many men out at once. He had been talking to the baker Tom Coxhell up the street. Coxhell had been nominated as captain for the match and had agreed to sail with the others.

'Is she safe to carry so many?' Senior Constable Murphy asked Hooper.

The fisherman assured the officer it would be okay. He explained with the nets removed he had plenty of room. He planned to bring in extra ballast – iron bars – to give the boat more stability. There is no record of whether or not Senior Constable Murphy, or anyone else, questioned the idea of the loose ballast. It is hard to believe the policeman didn't have some concerns about the planned trip. After all, everyone knew what had happened in Western Port at that terrible Hastings regatta just two years earlier.

Thirty-one

It was late afternoon, New Year's Day in 1890. A regatta was underway in the Western Port town of Hastings, a half-day ride across the peninsula from Mornington. Boats were being sailed in preparation for the following day's race. Wind was light. One of these racers, called *Albert*, was about two miles from the jetty.

There was no rush or panic in her crew: two brothers from suburban Cheltenham, Albert and George Whitehead, and two local fishermen, Sebastian Orsino and George Sheay. The boat was being well sailed until a hefty squall made her jolt and shudder. The Whitehead brothers let the sheets go but the mainsail stalled and took the wind's full punch. The iron ballast shot across beneath their feet and crashed leeward (downwind), causing the whole vessel to tip so the mast was suddenly touching the water. The boat filled like a cup in a sink and began falling slowly toward the bottom of the bay. The brothers, Orsino and Sheay were left bobbing.

Other boats survived the squall and were sailed over to the wreck by their skippers, who would be rescuers.

Having come from homes closer to Melbourne, neither of the Whiteheads were expert swimmers, whereas Sheay and Orsino dived and moved across the surface like seals.

Sheay realised his feet were entangled in ropes, which were going to drown him. If he had panicked he would have died within a minute. But he was composed and able to free himself before he swallowed too much water. He made for one of the boats, climbed to safety and spluttered in relief.

Albert and George Whitehead could only thrash to stay afloat. Their arms were slowing through exhaustion. Orsino had to decide whether to risk death by going to the brothers, or swim for another boat. He chose to go to them.

Both brothers grabbed Orsino as if he were a buoy and, without malice, pushed him under. He couldn't hold them both. Orsino freed himself, dived under and came up beneath Albert, holding him in a way that threatened neither of them. George, without any energy, went limp and drowned. Orsino had chosen the other brother, perhaps only because he was easier to manage. Sheay and the other boats' skippers helped the surviving Whitehead and Orsino climb to safety. Orsino dived with a rope and fastened it to the sunken *Albert*. The squall-hit yacht was dragged to land.

Hundreds of shocked witnesses, including Whitehead relatives and friends, stood mute on the shore as the local policeman requisitioned a boat and rigged it with a drag; after a grim hour or two of searching the bottom of the bay, George's body was found and lifted into the recovery craft. Several seamen helped carry the corpse from the jetty onto the back of a carriage, whose horse was urged to go slowly to the railway station, followed by dozens of crying people. Such a cortege, led by wet, grieving brother Albert Whitehead, had never been seen in Hastings and formed a memory to last a lifetime.

A note ran in the local newspaper, the *South Bourke and Mornington Journal*, with some of the details of the accident. Sebastian Orsino was nominated for a bravery award.

> To all swimmers it must be apparent that nothing but the most heroic conduct of Mr Orsino could have rescued the drowning man from a watery grave, and it is one of those cases of singularly brave and unselfish behavior that deserves ever to be remembered; for a man, who regardless of his own life and with a wife and family dependent on him, strives to save the life of a human creature deserves the highest award from the Humane Society and some acknowledgement from the people of the locality.

The deeds of Orsino were recounted for weeks in the district and recalled in print several times. It is not possible residents of the regatta-loving Mornington did not know about the accident and its cause. There were lessons in George Whitehead's death if anyone was willing to learn.

Thirty-two

On the Friday afternoon before the long weekend, Willie Caldwell stood among thousands of others on the banks of the fast-moving Yarra River to watch the twenty-fifth annual Public Schools Boat Race. Scotch College was host in charge of the event and all former pupils were keen to come along and barrack for the four-man crew wearing the brightest uniform, up against teams from Geelong and Melbourne Grammar and Wesley College.

Willie had adored his time at Scotch and took pride in its successes. Also, his good friend Norman Young was one of the oarsmen.

In his senior year at 'good old Scotch' Willie had been a leader of the school's esteemed cadet corps, winning the prestigious 'Lady Loch colours', for performing drills under competition rules better than any in the colony. Under the charge of drill master Captain Whitehead, who wore long hanging mutton chops and a pout, Scotch was said to have 'ranked in efficiency with the First Battalion of the Victorian Militia'. The students didn't only march in time; they practised war games at muddy campgrounds (called 'encampments'). They were often held at Langwarrin, not far from The Point, and on special occasions Willie, one of Captain Whitehead's favourites, was allowed to sleep in his bed at the manse on Sunday nights before catching the train back to school.

Lady Loch, wife of Lord Loch (Governor of Victoria), designed the 'colours and trophies' to be won by the public school with the best cadets. In 1890, Willie Caldwell went with the other cadets to a ceremony at Government House in Collins Street to accept the colours.

'We fellows were pleased and so was the good doctor,' Willie told his family, referring to the esteemed Scotch principal, Dr Alexander Morrison. 'He made us a speech in his best Scotch and praised us all up, and looked as pleased as Punch.'

A photo survives of the Scotch boys with their prize from Lady Loch. Captain Whitehead was standing at the back with Dr Morrison. Willie Caldwell was lying on his side, as relaxed as if he were awaiting arrival of a cup of tea, his young face under a slouch hat in a pose of satisfaction bordering on cockiness. A scribe from that era might have said he was the image of manliness. Norman Young was the other boy lying on the ground.

From that proud day Willie might have pursued a military career. He had been given the rank of lieutenant in the Victoria Volunteer Cadet Corps, but he knew he had to give up 'soldiering' if he were to be a doctor.

On leaving Scotch he went to Captain Whitehead and told him of his plans. Captain Whitehead was disappointed and told Willie he had the 'makings of a fine soldier'.

'Any time you want to take it up again, come to me and I will do what I can for you,' he said to the graduate.

Willie explained, 'My father wishes me to give all my time to my studies while at the university.'

Then he started at Ormond College, where he found himself looking up to another school master, Sir John Henry MacFarland. Willie once said of his new mentor, 'You can't help understanding anything Mr MacFarland instructs you in. He puts it so clearly. He is just the man to be the head of a college like Ormond. He never interferes with the students in any way, if he can possibly help it, but appears to hardly notice us when we are out of our classes.'

Medical students were known for their 'rowdiness' at plays and other social events in the city. By all accounts, Willie wasn't a boisterous ringleader. Instead, he was a typical 'masher', or ladies' man.

Close observers of Willie Caldwell as he stood on the banks of the Yarra to watch the race on that Friday afternoon would have noted he wore his Scotch coloured ribbons pinned to his jacket with an Ormond tie.

Since 1868, Scotch had won ten of the boat races, while Geelong had won nine. Rumour had it the lads from Geelong had again picked a dauntingly strong team.

The race was a mile and a quarter long, upstream from the 'mouth of the canal' to 'Ferrars Street'. Of course the race was an English tradition rebadged for the Australian schools. Emphasis was given to colours: Geelong wore 'Cambridge blue'; Melbourne chose 'Oxford blue'; Wesley donned blue and white, and Scotch was glowing in 'cardinal'.

A gun signalled the start of the event. Some spectators watched from a small steamer, closely following the rowers. From his vantage, Willie could see the grammar schools side by side, with Scotch heading out to a boat's length lead, and Wesley falling behind. Willie might have wondered for a second, where was his old Wesleyan mate, Charlie? Geelong made its move late in the race, but by then the Cardinals were cruising too far ahead. The old boys cheered and hoorayed.

At this time – about a quarter to four – Willie had not decided he'd go home to Mornington for the weekend. In fact, he was more likely to stay in Melbourne. Norman Young had told his parents he might be bringing Willie to visit them at their house in Elsternwick, a southern suburb. Willie, who had been given four days off by Ormond, had even written to Rev. Caldwell saying not to expect him.

Over the long weekend, he was planning to do some study, at least. The second-year medical students were due to soon work in hospitals and he wanted to be up with all his learning. Also, Willie and Norman, who were as close in friendship as Hugh and Charlie, had talked about going into the city for some fun. But now Willie was not sure. He hadn't heard whether Jim was home but there was a chance he might be.

An hour later, the sun was falling over The Point, leaving behind a pink sky: the promise of a fine Saturday. The Caldwell family had gathered in the breakfast room.

Hugh, Jim, Alice, and the little ones Jack, Jeannie and Sallie were sitting on six cane chairs around a table. A fire was burning, warming one side of the room more than the other. The walls were decorated with pictures and books. This was the best room in the house. The dining room was grander, with its sideboard, tall armchairs, chiffonier and organ. The drawing room, where Rev. Caldwell was now sitting alone on his sofa beside the piano and his 'afternoon' tea table, was beautiful and formal. But the breakfast room was where the laughter of siblings had soaked into the carpet and fallen into the cracks of the bookshelf, and sometimes snuck out the swinging door, into the high hall, and throughout the family home.

Hugh was telling a story about Willie and Charlie, how the three of them had gone together to the Agricultural Show in Melbourne last August and missed the last train to Mornington, walking from Frankston after midnight. Alice reminded them that Charlie had stayed the night, instead of daring to wake the Allchins. Needing a bed, he had hopped in with 'little Jack'.

'In *my* bed,' laughed Jack at the memory.

Alice recalled with a chuckle, 'I popped my head in the boys' room that morning and saw Charlie and thought he was Jack.'

'We slept way past breakfast that day and didn't even make it to church,' Hugh said.

Then came a laugh from outside the breakfast room door. It was the same musical laugh they knew only belonged to Willie. The door opened and he showed his face but only for an instant, before disappearing again to place his overcoat and hat by the front door.

'Willie?' Alice said.

'Old Bill,' said Jim.

The little ones froze in anticipation.

Jim didn't think Willie had seen or heard him so he slid under the table to trick him on his return. It had been months since they had seen each other down at Tasmania, when Willie was throwing tarts into teacups. Hugh covered Jim with the tablecloth.

Willie came into the room with a broad grin.

'Well, old lady, how are you?' he asked Alice and kissed her. 'Where is he?' Willie demanded to know.

'Who do you mean?' Alice said.

Like a kid hiding under a bed from Mummy, Jim stayed silent behind the tablecloth. Willie and Hugh shook hands.

'Jim, of course,' Willie said.

Alice replied, 'He is still away in Gippsland.'

'Oh, that's alright,' said Willie. 'But I saw the mater [Marian] in the hall, and she told me Jim was here.'

He peered under the table to find his older brother, giggling.

'Come out of that, you beggar,' said Old Bill. They shook hands and held on for a second longer, enjoying each other's grip.

Jim told Willie he looked better than the last time they'd met.

'You don't look so white,' he said.

Willie told him if he had looked pale it was because he had been slicing open cadavers. 'It was a shock to my system.'

Jack asked Willie why he was wearing his Scotch 'colours'.

'Old Scotch won,' he said, recounting the boat race.

Alice frowned. 'Willie, I shall always regret that I have not a photograph of you taken in your regimentals.'

'Ah, wait until you get one of me in my academical dress,' he said. Alice had seen him in his 'gown and trencher' but preferred his military-style uniform.

Just then Rev. Caldwell came into the room. For a man of little emotion, he seemed moved. He stood with his three elder sons by the hearth. Alice noticed for the first time her father was shorter than Jim, Willie and Hugh. His back was slightly curved. The minister looked to warm up and snuck closest to the fire.

It was a reunion to savour and the conversation stretched late. At some point, someone said, 'What a pity Tom is not over from Tasmania.'

Thirty-three

Saturday came with a light breeze and few clouds. Charles Hooper went to the harbour early and looked out from the cliffs at the bay's gently shifting shades of blue and knew it was a fine day for a sail. He began making final preparations to the *Process*. It was a relatively quiet morning, almost lazy. There were usually about fifteen commercial fishing crews based in Mornington, but most of the bigger vessels had gone to Port Albert for the weekend in search of whiting, pike and garfish.

Before sailing through The Heads toward Bass Strait, the skippers of those boats might have noted the Melbourne Observatory's recent 'weather telegram' (posted three o'clock Friday afternoon), which read:

> Barometer steady, fine but cloudy, moderate fresh west winds and rough seas. Port Phillip to Wilson's Promontory, barometer steady, cloudy, squally, showery. Fresh WNW winds and moderate seas.

Late morning, Hooper and the few other fishermen left at The Point stopped what they were doing and watched as an elegant visitor with mighty white sails made its way toward them from the bay's northern tip. It was the famous *Wanderer*.

The *Wanderer*'s owner, Henry Penketh Fergie was a public 'notary'. Born and raised in Liverpool, he came to Australia in 1854, aged twenty-five, and went on to become a conveyancer, money lender, local government councillor and Justice of the Peace. During the 1880s land boom, he had expanded his interests, speculating on large farming stations in New South Wales and acting as a lobbyist for the newly formed Melbourne Tramway and Omnibus Company.

Fergie was famous for his sailing adventures, overseas and along the Victoria coastline. His craft was just as well known. Built in 1880 and launched in 1882, the *Wanderer* boasted a fifty-foot-high mainmast; her sails spread 1400 square feet. The sailing elite reckoned Fergie's new craft was the finest cutter-yacht of her size in the Southern Hemisphere.

In 1889, Fergie and his favourite sailing mate, Melbourne-based architect Arthur Peck, had made national headlines when they sailed *Wanderer* back to her home state of South Australia and suffered damage in high winds off Port Adelaide. Peck had to row to land in a dinghy to raise the alarm and organise a rescue. The yacht was fixed and sailed back to Victoria, despite 'disagreeable conditions', where she was increasingly used on pleasant weekend bay trips.

Fergie had brought Peck and several other Melbourne businessmen with him to Mornington for the Queen's Birthday holiday. The menu for the weekend read:

Dinner:

Oysters au naturel / Spring chicken / Cold roast teal / Pickled pork

Vegetables:

Green peas / Cauliflower / Turnips

Sweets:

Plum pudding / Pastry / Cheese / Olives

Dessert:

Fruits in season / Lollies / Coffee

Wines:

Champagne / Claret / Whiskey / Beer

It would be quite a party aboard the *Wanderer*. Hooper and the other fishermen might have noticed that, on arrival, Fergie was serving whiskey and soda to his guests. With a promise of vermouth by 1 pm.

Thirty-four

Main Street was as busy as it could be on a weekend outside summer. Now on its third day without rain, the town looked clean and lovely. Cobblestone gutters were clear. Puddles had dried and the reddish gravel road had been rolled hard. All the buildings from the boom period were now up and had been unchanged for a year or so, giving the village centre a lived-in maturity it had never previously claimed.

The last of the improvements – an extension of the police headquarters – had belatedly been finished. Senior Constable Murphy had overseen the renovation of the grounds, which became dramatic when a human skeleton was unearthed during the digging of foundations. At first, it was thought the bones had belonged to a European settler. But they were so neatly placed in the earth, the remains could only have been from the Boon Wurrung.

The footpaths were full of shoppers, strollers and talkers. Residents were moving with an unhurried air of four-days-off-work satisfaction. However, one young man was in a hurry. It was John Kinna. The telegraph operator was striding into the bootmaker Thomas Hutchinson's workshop; he had left it until the last hour to pick up one of his football boots. His sole had needed repairing after the game against the Rovers.

In a conversation that barely lasted thirty seconds, Hutchinson handed over the fixed boot. He commented that it still had a mark on the toe.

'I could fix that with more time,' the cobbler said.

Kinna said thanks but maybe another time. He needed to wear his boots today, against Mordialloc. Hutchinson wished him luck and watched him take off through the front of the shop and in the direction of his home.

Thirty-five

Hugh finished work at J.D. Grover's workshop at half past eleven, two hours earlier than he would have if the football match were being played at home. He benched his tools and ran out via the timber yard. His sports-loving boss understood better than anyone the excitement of the hours before a big match. He was happy enough for his apprentice to rush off even if his business' productivity might take a glancing blow. Grover would soon close up shop anyway and head to the railway station. He wanted to be among the barrackers in Mordialloc. A train was leaving at two o'clock.

Hugh ran all the way home and went straight into the breakfast room. The first person he saw was Jim, smoking his pipe with Willie.

'Are you coming today?' he asked his older brother.

Jim was coy and shrugged. He seemed contented after a morning spent riding his young horse at the beach.

Willie asked when the boat was leaving. Hugh told him it would be soon.

Hooper had instructed all the players on Thursday night the *Process* would need to leave the jetty at midday or not long after. The match was scheduled for three o'clock.

'I say, Bill, are you coming to the match?' Hugh asked. 'You'd better. We're sure to be short of men, making the early start, so come along and give us a hand.'

Willie was in. No worries. He hadn't worn the local colours since those matches against Frankston the previous season.

The two younger brothers then tried to convince Jim to come with them. As if time didn't matter, Jim turned to look out the window at the sky. 'Will it be fine?' he asked.

Alice came into the room as Hugh assured Jim the weather was friendly. Willie said it would be a great chance to 'get one back' for Mornington, having lost to Mordialloc in the last match of 1891.

Jim was quiet. Alice spoke on his behalf, her words muffled by her cold. 'Willie, it's all very well for you. You will be playing in the match, and enjoying yourself, and, besides, that will keep you warm, but it is a different matter to Jim; he will have nothing to do, but stand looking on, shivering in the cold.'

Alice suspected Jim would go anyway. After breakfast, she'd seen him and Willie kicking a ball in the front garden with young Jack. How could he resist going with his brothers, she questioned. But she wanted him to stay, to keep her company.

'Indeed,' Willie said, voice rising. 'If he comes he will have to play too. There will be no standing about shivering in the cold, I can tell you.'

'But can you play?' asked Alice of Jim.

She knew Jim hadn't played in a game since the 1880s. But he was not an old man. He was twenty-one and as fit as any. His endurance forged through long days on the axe had moulded him into the ideal athlete.

'I used to be able to when I was at Walker's,' Jim said, referring to his time at state school, five years earlier. 'I dare say I could play a bit, though I am out of practice.'

He was now apparently warming to the prospect of surprising any doubters.

Hugh and Willie saw the clock and said they couldn't wait to change. They bounded upstairs to find their uniforms and boots. Hugh sought a light jacket and overcoat, knowing layers would be as important as shields against the bay's cold breath. Willie rugged up, too. He grabbed an old Gladstone bag, something to hold their clothes while they played.

It was about this time Willie asked Hugh if Charlie was coming to the match. Hugh nodded. He had sent a telegram to Charlie to tell him he should hop off the train at Mordialloc.

Back in the breakfast room, Alice told Jim he had better make up his mind quickly. She wanted to plead with him to stay and thought about asking if he would take her for an afternoon ride. But she felt it inevitable he would want to be with his brothers. 'You are sure to go in the end,' she said.

Jim rose and exhaled. His one last thought was that the horses needed feeding. But they were in a lush paddock.

'Yes, I am sure to go in the end.'

He went upstairs and found some warm clothes. He had no knickerbockers but trousers would do for the game. Someone from the committee would bring a spare jersey.

Alice and the little ones finished making dinner for the footballers, while Rev. Caldwell, as usual, sat alone in the drawing room, writing tomorrow's sermon. He would have heard only murmurs from the other room.

Alice was kneeling on the hearth-rug, about to pour some boiling water into the teapot, when Willie appeared and offered help.

'I am quite used to it, you know,' he said. Apparently Willie was the tea maker at the Ormond dormitory. Jim came in and they all drank tea and ate a large meal of meat, carved by Hugh.

'Look here, you fellows, you ought to consider yourselves highly honoured,' he boasted.

'You are a brick,' one of his brothers said.

They all laughed.

Alice, Jeannie, Jack and Sallie waited on them, topping up their cups and plates. Silence took over, save for the clanging of cutlery and some slurping. Hughie spoke next and suggested they eat as much as possible, given they didn't know what time they would eat again.

The children's stepmother, Marian, popped into the room and reminded Jeannie, the eldest of the little ones, of the tarts they had made. The sweets were still in the oven but ready for eating. Jeannie picked four tarts and placed them on a plate.

Jim laughed, 'You might have given us warning so we could leave room for tarts.'

They each took one and scoffed it down. Jeannie went to Hugh with the leftover but he surprised her by saying he was full.

'No thanks, I really could not eat it, not even to oblige you.'

'Willie?' Jeannie said, her bottom lip falling.

'I could not possibly, Jeannie. I don't know when I ate so much before.'

'Jim, will you have it?' the small chef asked.

'Jeannie,' he said. 'I have had a good square meal but I am not going to be done by that much.' He took it and ate it for the taste alone.

Seconds later the lads stood up and went to their overcoats in the hall.

Alice yearned to kiss them goodbye but didn't want to give them her sniffle. She did not fear for them on the bay and was glad they were going to spend a day together. She smiled and waved as they went along the hall.

Jim, Willie and Hugh Caldwell then walked out the door, down the steps and past the gate, toward the bay. Watching them every step through the drawing-room window was their papa, lifting his gaze from the page for a moment to admire his sons, who had once wrestled as children in the same yard they were now leaving behind.

While eating his own dinner and tart an hour or so later, Rev. Caldwell asked Alice where the lads had gone. On finding out, he complained about Jim going with the others because he had wanted him to take care of the animals, including the old carthorse Kitty.

'If none of the boys are here, I will have to do it myself,' he concluded.

Thirty-six

Charlie went to work on Saturday morning, from his lodgings in the South Yarra Coffee Palace to the office in Swanston Street, carrying his bag of football gear and a few other belongings. His corner of the city was quieter than usual but he surely heard the murmuring crowd in nearby Collins Street, where people came dressed in their sharpest clobber to wander along the footpaths at the 'Paris end'. 'Doing the Block,' as it was called, had been a Saturday morning ritual in Melbourne since the sixties and continued even through those dark Depression years.

Novelist Fergus Hume gave perhaps the truest depiction of life in the city at this time in his book *The Mystery of a Hansom Cab*, published in 1893. For research, Hume peered into Melbourne's back street hovels *and* watched the elite, or would-be elite, strutting up and down Collins.

> It was Saturday morning and fashionable Melbourne was 'doing the Block'. Collins Street is to the Southern city what

> Bond and the Row are in London . . . Portly merchants, forgetting Flinders Lane and incoming ships, walked beside pretty daughters; and the representatives of swelldom were stalking along in their customary apparel of burly brimmed hats, high collars and immaculate suits.

Charlie must have been used to catching this scene. What young bloke could resist leering at the lyrebird set? Though it's doubtful he did it this day. He had to finish his work and leave early for the Melbourne Terminus, just a short walk away, and catch a train to Mordialloc.

The architecture trade was not as hot as it used to be. His boss, Alfred Dunn, was still at the top of his profession but Charlie wondered whether the economic crisis was going to catch up with him, as it was with other men of real estate. English-born Dunn had tried to enter politics a few months earlier but failed. Was he overinvested? Is that why he was trying to shift into public life?

Charlie had been fortunate to be articled to Mr Dunn, a handsome, stylish and wealthy prince of his industry, who had won many competitions for his 'sensitivity and appreciation of an Australian style'. In the past decade Dunn had designed buildings along Collins Street, on the corner of Swanston and Little Collins streets (later known as Town Hall Chambers), coffee palaces throughout Victoria and New South Wales (including Broken Hill – still standing as the tourist friendly Palace Hotel) and several Wesleyan churches. By the time Charlie had graduated from Wesley College and joined Alfred Dunn's firm in 1889, the architect had become a fellow to admire.

How Charlie came to work for Dunn is unclear. But there appears to be a link between the celebrated architect and the Allchin family beyond their shared Wesleyan faith. In 1888 Dunn had designed a building in Mornington for a well-to-do auctioneer, Hon. Robert Byrne. Dunn also had to source bricks for the project – from the Allchin clay pit. The architect employed Charlie a year after Mr Byrne's house was built. Dunn liked the boy for his manners and work ethic. Ultimately, Charlie wanted to be a civil engineer and Dunn was going to help him achieve his aim.

But the trainee was not obsessed with work. And every Saturday, at about noon, he left what he was doing at Dunn's offices, carried his packed bag into Swanston Street, across Flinders Street and over to the train terminus.

On Saturday 21 May, he followed this routine as punctually as ever, dressed in a suit, with the hint of a thin, new moustache. He was seven days from turning twenty. What better way to celebrate than spending a few days back home with friends and family?

Thirty-seven

Most of the Mornington team had gathered on the jetty beside the *Process*. 'Here they come,' someone shouted and all turned to see the smiling trio of Caldwells approaching.

Most of the men knew each other, although Jim Caldwell had to introduce himself to half the side. Hooper's fishing colleague, Coomber, was joining the team for his first game. Everybody except Jim knew his face, if not his name. Another man making his debut for the club was Charles Williams, son of local carpenter Stephen Williams. (Actually, Charles' real name was Stephen Charles Smith Williams but he was known by his second given name, perhaps to differentiate from his father.) Charles was twenty-three; his family had lived in the district for decades, with a home at nearby Moorooduc since the early 1860s.

The players were similarly dressed in dark blue and grey woollen trousers, serge or tweed, flannel shirts, waistcoats, overcoats, and soft hats or caps.

The party seemed at ease. Perhaps the only player not relaxed at this point was the baker Tom Coxhell. As match captain, it was Coxhell's job to count heads and make sure he had enough players to field a team. Hugh told him about Charlie's plans. That meant he needed nineteen more players. At that moment he knew they were a few short. He told the boys to pile in so he could count them one final time.

Coxhell was a seasoned and respected member of the team. He had been born and raised in Mornington and now ran a business in Main Street. His parents had been in town as long as the Allchins; in fact, his mother had arrived in Australia a month earlier than Sarah Allchin (then Jagger) at the end of 1855.

Theresa Anne Coxhell (nee Tynan) was born in 1831 and came to The Point from Dublin. She worked for a year at the Briars for Alexander Balcombe as a 'ladies' maid'. By 1857 she had married Thomas Coxhell, an Englishman brick-maker. They had eight children over the next twenty years. John Thomas (Tom) Coxhell was their fourth born. Tom was now twenty-six years old. He was married to a lady named Eleanor (nee Cotter) and they had one baby, Cecelia, born in 1890. All the Coxhells had bred well and spread throughout the shire; little Cecelia had no fewer than twenty-two cousins.

So it wasn't a stretch for Tom Coxhell to organise a boatful of footballers, but he did look stressed. Perhaps he was thinking about leaving Eleanor and Cecelia alone for the afternoon and evening. Or maybe he was concerned about the dangers of the trip. If so, he did not say anything.

The players made themselves as comfortable as they could. Coxhell pointed to each man, counting as he went. Hooper's son Charles was preparing the sails. There was Coomber, the Caldwells – standing together – and John Kinna. Henry Short, the bank manager, had arrived. He was standing beside his accountant William Grover (son of J. D.) and his uncle, also William.

'Here's Coles,' someone said.

Willie Coles was arriving just in time. He was carrying a trunk and looked very soldierly in his army coat, the same uniform James Firth had on.

'What's that?' someone asked of the trunk's contents.

Beaming with pride, Coles stepped down into the *Process*. Then opened his luggage to reveal a polished cornet. A cheer went up and Coles played a few notes in celebration.

Standing beside Coles were two teenagers, Firth and Alfred Lawrence. Firth was only seventeen but looked five years older, owing to his bulk. He was even thicker set than Coles. Firth and Coles were firm friends, having both served in the Victorian Rangers on training exercises.

The Firth family was one of the oldest in the district. James' father, John, born in the remote Orkney Islands, off the Scottish coast, had arrived in Australia as a young man and made his name as a farmer in the town of Somerville. He married a Schnapper Point local, Catherine Heffernan, and they had five children. James was their second born. On leaving school, James Firth had taken an apprenticeship with the well-known blacksmith and wheelwright John Jenkins. Young Firth was apparently handy with a hammer and had the meatiest forearms as proof.

Lawrence, who appeared a mere boy in comparison, was just as recognisable in town as Firth. Alfred Herbert

Lawrence was the son of the storekeeper of the same name. Alfred senior was a Londoner before he came to Schnapper Point via Gippsland in the 1860s. He married Ann Roland, originally from Devonshire, and Alfred junior was the second of ten children. The Lawrence family store was the closest to the railway station. Their business also catered for special functions and the parents were often praised in the press for their food and beverage service.

Coxhell counted sixteen – including a P. Schultz, about whom little is known – although the boy Hooper was only thirteen and would not play the game. So there were fifteen footballers aboard. They could only hope a few more had gone to Mordialloc by train, or they would have to pluck some men from the crowd.

Anyway, time was running out and they had to leave. Coomber removed the rope tying the boat to the jetty and a few hands pushed them clear. Free floating in the harbour between the pier and jetty on one side, and the red bluff foreshore on the other, Hooper lowered the centreboard for stability and took his place at the helm, hands on the tiller. He told his fair-haired son and Coomber to hoist the gaff; players were instructed to stand or sit on the port (right) side.

It was crowded over there and not all could lean against the rails so some of the young men instead sat still on the thwart. Coomber, on starboard (left) side, lowered into a crouch and pulled firmly on the sheets, hand over hand, raising the sails. He had not quite finished when a man from the shore shouted out from the jetty.

'Hey there, Hooper, you missed a couple.'

Two more footballers had turned up: Tom Hutchins, the

fisherman from nearby Balcombe Creek and William Cavell. Both were regular players. Cavell had been one of the better performers in the Rovers match two weeks earlier. Hutchins was known to be a fine runner, having recently won a 130-yard dash at the Sorrento sports day.

They bellowed again for the *Process* to return but Hooper refused because it was considered unlucky to 'put back' and start a journey twice. Hutchins and Cavell had to decide whether to catch the train to Mordialloc or abandon their footballing plans for the week. They walked back to Main Street, Hutchins on his way to the train station, Cavell home.

Back on the bay, the sails were up but not yet full of wind. On request from Hooper, Coomber and the skipper's son had tied – reefed – the lower part of the mainsail against the boom. This meant the canvas was not as broad as it could be. Hooper was being cautious to give the players the gentlest ride up the coast, at least at the beginning.

There was banter and nervous excitement among the footballers. Hooper positioned the *Process* so she was pointing back at the jetty. The sails were still flapping like flags. Then the captain announced he was 'bearing away'. By changing course, he found the breeze, the sails filled and the boat started slicing through the sea, leaving fizzing foam in her wake.

They were on their way to Mordialloc.

Thirty-eight

After a few minutes, the captain, crew and passengers relaxed into the trip. Most of the players sat comfortably up on the windward side decks, the breeze behind them; they were acting as 'live ballast', helping balance the craft. From their positions they had a lovely sight of rock cliffs and calm inlets, all the way to Frankston.

In the shadowed pools of this part of the coast swim schools of varied species – red southern goatfish, slit-mouthed scalyfin, sea sweep, zebra fish, magpie perch and long-finned pike – above a floor of coloured sponges and corals as pretty as any flower garden, home to seahorses and thousands of starfish.

Cruising as they were now in a consistent breeze blowing at them from the centre of the bay, the players would not have seen the smaller fish but it's likely they noticed some wildlife – a stingray, dolphins or jelly fish, or the squid that float near the surface of Mount Eliza's most isolated beaches.

There were other boats out. Fishermen were still working in the area. The Allchin family's trade ketch *Maggie* was making a run to Melbourne that afternoon and was likely heading to the city for stores at this hour. But no one later mentioned seeing Captain Jack Bunn so maybe he was further up the bay.

As the *Process* neared Frankston, almost halfway to Mordialloc, the footballers started singing. Willie Coles was the music man. He fetched his cornet and played some of the era's most popular songs. A favourite knee-slapper was *The Parson and Clerk*, a comic tune that always had singers laughing between lines.

> Oh, a parson prayed to his flock one day, on the sins of the human race.
> And the clerk, 'Amen,' aloud did say, with the solemnest tone and face.
> And the pious clerk, in the quiet thought, did venture a bit or remark.
> 'All sin is sweet,' said the parson. 'Then sin is for me,' said the clerk.
> Amen.
> 'Oh sin is for me,' said the clerk.

Coles played this one at all the concerts in town. Many townsfolk would have remembered his rendition at the club fundraiser back in 1889, which 'evoked quite a thunder of applause'. Those who didn't know the words at least shouted 'Amen'.

> 'Oh the boys are awfully tribulous,' the parson he says with a groan.
> 'And the boys too oft at Sunday school won't let the young hussies alone.
> And I've watched the boys behind their books, I've seen the boys their larks.
> They're kissing the girls,' said the parson. 'I've done it myself,' said the clerk.
> Amen
> 'And they're fond of it too,' said the clerk.

Laughter and clapping followed. Then came a request for Coles to play another song.

Hooper still had the reefs on the sails when the wind began to drop. The team was about to leave behind the cliffs near Frankston and head for deeper water, to avoid the shallow, sandy beaches that lined the coast the rest of the way to Mordialloc. But the *Process* was slowing, almost stalling. Hooper mentioned to Coomber they might need to 'shake out' the reefs to gather more wind.

Coles used the calmest of weather to play a slow and whimsical folk song that will be remembered forever as the soundtrack to the Mornington boys' journey. It was called 'The Ship That Never Returned' and all knew it because the same song was heard on the doomed ship *Gambier* before it went down.

There had been an infamous head-on crash in Port Phillip the previous winter, involving two steamers *Gambier* and *Easby* as they were attempting to pass through The Heads. Neither slowed down, nor gave way. They collided in the western channel of the bay's entrance. Both captains later swore they did not see the other coming in time to evade. The last words heard by anyone before the crash were men from both ships calling, 'Stop her, stop her.' Then the madness began.

The smaller *Easby*, carrying a load of fruit, slammed into the *Gambier* near the bridge. It was a savage body shot, which cut her down. Had the *Gambier* floated longer it might have been easy to ground her at the edge of the channel and few would have died but it went down too quickly. Seven minutes.

On the day of the accident, the iron ferry *Gambier* had left Sydney and was to drop off passengers in Melbourne. She was carrying twenty-nine people in saloon class and thirty-eight in steerage. Altogether there were 103 people aboard when she sank.

The captain of *Gambier* told the Court of Marine Inquiry:

> In what little time there was to be spared for such a purpose we got out a boat and the ladies were placed in it. I had to take to the seas, and was swimming around for fully a quarter of an hour before I was noticed.

The *Easby* skipper belatedly sent lifeboats and saved as many passengers as he could, earning praise, though he was later blamed for causing the accident.

Smaller boats from the *Gambier* flipped as passengers and crew tried to seat the women. Some were saved but others drowned in the chop. Those who could swim had a chance. The mayhem killed as many as the temperature of the sea.

The *Gambier*'s engine manager – 'donkeyman' – James Bell said of being stranded in the water, 'The night was beautifully clear, and as I was keeping myself afloat I could see the lights of Queenscliff [the nearest town] as plain as possible. When I was picked up and placed in one of the lifeboats I noticed that there was a lady passenger lying in the boat and foaming at the mouth.'

Twenty-three people died in about ten minutes.

The *Argus* newspaper reported on Saturday 29 August that before the crash, right up until midnight, there was music on the *Gambier*, so passengers could pass time and stop from falling asleep.

> Strangely enough, among the songs which were sung was one called 'The Ship That Never Returned'. By melancholy coincidence the singer, a young man named Johnston, was drowned a few hours later when almost in sight of the port.

Young men don't spook easily and there was no hint of mournfulness or trepidation in the voices of the Mornington team when they sang the words over Willie Coles' searching notes.

> On a summer day, as the waves were rippling
> By the soft and gentle breeze
> Did a ship set sail with her cargo laden
> For a port beyond the seas. Did she ever return?
> No she never returned
> And her fate was yet unlearned
> Tho' for years and years there were fond ones waiting
> For the ship that never returned.

Hooper, who had waited long enough for the breeze to pick back up, told his son and Coomber to undo the reefing ties. The full racing sails were revealed and the *Process* immediately began moving faster. It was the end of the pleasant sail. The wind strengthened as the footballers headed north. So began an hour of hold-your-cap, salt-in-your-eyes fun. Now the *Process* could stick the ball under her arm, hitch back her shoulders and lean forward – chest out – at full regatta speed. The players were on the rail, belly-laughing at the motion and talking about the things young men do when they are free and together.

Football was one topic of discussion. But, with sixteen personalities aboard, it would have been unlikely the talk centred on local sport for too long. No doubt someone, at some moment, would have mentioned the sharks that had been sighted along the beaches they were now passing. The previous spring, bathers were taking their 'morning ablution' in the open bay when someone shouted 'Shark!' and witnesses turned to see fish no shorter than 'twenty feet'.

The twenty-footer was not the strangest sighting along those beaches over summer. In December strollers found washed ashore a dead horse, fallen from a boat on the way to or from the metropolis.

The team would surely have talked, if only briefly, about the murderer Frederick Deeming, due to be hanged by the end of the long weekend. The latest news, as far as the boys knew, was that Deeming's defence counsel had appealed his sentence to the Privy Council in London. It was a desperate last attempt to avoid the noose. But it had not worked. Maybe one or two of the players were planning to go to Melbourne Gaol for the event. Thousands were expected.

More likely, they were planning a day trip on Tuesday – the actual Queen's Birthday – to one of the big Victorian Football Association matches in the city. The league was staging five special games at eleven o'clock and another two at three o'clock. The crowds would be enormous.

That Saturday afternoon the VFA was organising a full round. Last year's champion Essendon was playing Richmond at Jolimont; powerhouse Carlton was due to meet Port Melbourne at the Melbourne Cricket Club ground; former league-heavyweight South Melbourne was hosting another top-three team, Fitzroy; Williamstown was welcoming Melbourne to its home oval: St Kilda was up against the new team Collingwood; and Geelong was to start favourite against Footscray because of its hometown advantage.

The Mornington lads would try to read about these matches before that night. It was their ritual after play to have tea at home and walk through the township together, or in small groups, to buy the evening papers and see how the 'Melbourne matches' had gone.

No one loved this part of the week more than Hugh and Charlie, who always went back to the Caldwell kitchen for tea and buttered toast piled atop the largest plate in the house. The servants had Saturday nights off work, so the youngsters always had the kitchen to themselves. They could eat in the dining room but the kitchen was their favourite. Hugh would scoff more than half the food. Charlie never minded. He was the smaller of the friends and he filled up quicker.

Hugh, seated with his brothers aboard the *Process*, his back to the westerly wind, was looking forward to seeing his best friend. Perhaps they would go hunting tomorrow and not come home until Tuesday. They had all the time they wanted for their next adventure.

Their last trip had been a month ago, beginning before the torrents of Easter and ending as the land threatened to overflow. They'd packed light and left home at twilight. Their parents came to wave them goodbye and stuff biscuits and cakes in their saddlebags. The boys planned to meet one of Charlie's friends from Wesley College at Dromana, about ten miles away. It was Charlie's friend's job to bring stores: cans of meat, tea and bread.

Beyond Dromana the trio rode by moonlight across the peninsula, through twenty miles of forest, swamp and paddock, up and over the Arthur's Seat range. At Cape Schanck, in the echoes of the wild surf, they came to a shepherd's hut. It was a grey and wet morning. The hunters cooked breakfast and then slept til midday. For the next few days they barely rested and ate only two meals a day, so they could hunt longer. When they did sit down, they consumed tea and freshly killed game. If they had no energy to cook, they heated some porridge.

'Not gruel,' Hugh explained later to his family. 'Real stiff, solid porridge.'

The weather was tolerable for Charlie, Hugh and Charlie's friend until the final day, when it rained and rained and rained. By the time they returned to their accommodation they looked as if they had been dipped in the ocean. Hugh made a big fire to dry their pants and shirts. Instead of sitting naked, they dressed in some old castaway clothes that were gathering mould in the back corner of the hut. Charlie's friend was lucky to find an old shirt; Charlie wrapped himself in a sheet; Hugh stepped into a dirty pair of pants.

After dinner, they changed back into their dried, warm originals and rode home – in roaring rain, shivering all the way. Hugh and Charlie made it back to The Point at midnight. The Caldwell family would recall for many long years how happy Hugh and Charlie were on their return. The rain had never beaten them. Not even close. A fierce fire was going in the breakfast room and they drank tea until their eyes closed. Charlie woke later and went home to find his mother had prepared him another supper.

Next day, Charlie and Hugh met after dawn at the creek bed on the Caldwell property to fish for eels, laughing endlessly at the memory of a wet-headed Charlie wrapped in that dirty old sheet.

Thirty-nine

Approaching Mordialloc pier, Hooper told his crew to lower the sails. Almost all the players helped flake the falling canvas, folding it back and forth against the boom. Coomber lashed it off. Hooper steered them in.

Once the *Process* was steadied against the timber landing and tied up, players began stepping out, extending a hand to the next man. Willie Coles didn't need help carrying his trunk. All the men thanked Hooper for the 'ride' and everyone but the baker Tom Coxhell looked healthy; his face had taken on the colour of the mid-afternoon clouds. He would later concede, 'the only person suffering from seasickness . . . myself'.

About a dozen people had been standing on the pier waiting for the team. Charlie Allchin was among them. Hugh gave Charlie the biggest smile and motioned to Jim and Willie. They all shook hands; this was the first time in their lives they had all come together to play football. If they'd been at a picnic or a wedding they might have stood around and lit a smoke in conversation.

'Hurry up,' someone said. 'Don't waste time here.'

The voice belonged to Henry Short. He had already taken off his coat and trousers and dressed to play: knickerbockers, long socks and tight red-and-white-striped jersey over a white, long-sleeve shirt. Short was always considered a 'naturally impatient' man. Now he had reason to be. The trip had taken two-and-a-quarter hours. The game was due to start.

The Mornington teammates could see their opponents among a larger crowd awaiting them on the foreshore beside the Mordialloc Hotel. Hooper left his son to look after the *Process* and went with all the other footballers to the game.

'Well, hello!' they heard a man say.

Some of the players, including Charlie, the Caldwells, James Firth, Coles, Short and Coxhell recognised him as the local publican Thomas Rennison. Until the 1880s Rennison had been a long-time resident of Mornington, once owning the Royal Hotel (then called Schnapper Point Hotel). His family had settled on the peninsula as early as the Allchins.

One of the players said to Rennison during the afternoon, 'We know you better than you do us. My father said to give you his best.' Some of the other players introduced themselves.

Rennison was chuffed. He had fond memories of his time at The Point. He apparently looked at the players' faces, as a teacher might inspect a new intake of pupils, perhaps seeing in them the image of their parents, and felt moved to say, 'I'm proud of such a fine strapping lot of young fellows.'

The team had no chance to socialise but surely took in the town's most impressive structure: the pub. A businessman of impressive foresight, Rennison had bought the Mordialloc Hotel in the seventies and leased it out, making structural improvements every now and then. In late 1891, only six months earlier, he had taken it over from the previous manager and spent money completely renovating it.

Mordialloc had long been the Sleeping Beauty of Port Phillip villages. City folk used to know this spot on the coast as having one hotel 'of a very primitive character' and a few fishermen's houses. The expanding eighties gave it a new reputation as a popular southern suburb of Melbourne complemented by holiday villas and a popular horseracing track called Epsom. Rennison's two-storey, grand-façade hotel had been improved to accommodate the regularly visiting racing crowd and a more affluent local population.

But on Saturday afternoons when the races weren't on, the locals went to the football. The Mordialloc Football Club was in its second year. The team had done well enough in its first season, playing sixteen matches, winning six (including a belting of Mornington), losing nine and drawing one. Admirably, the new mob had kicked fifty-three goals and conceded only forty-eight. Goal sneak Ernest Millman had been leading scorer.

A practice match for the 1892 campaign had been held between members of the Mordialloc club on 16 April at 'Rennison's Field', named because it was beside his hotel. Rennison had even built a pavilion for barrackers to shelter from the wind that made it past the foreshore scrub. Mordialloc had then played three proper matches, including a victory over the suburban Caulfield club. The locals would start as favourites against Mornington.

Twenty young men from The Point – those who had arrived by boat plus five others – changed quickly into their playing uniforms and walked onto the field as one. Rennison's Field looked magnificent in the late-autumn sunshine. It had been roped off so over-keen spectators wouldn't wander on. Beyond the boundary there were two flags flying: a new one for the Mordialloc Football Club and a Union Jack. Not far away was a handful of men, women and children from Mornington, who had come to barrack for an upset.

Forty

The game was called off at 5.30 pm, both teams having scored two goals. No match report was ever written. Often a draw feels like a loss. But this time it must have delivered the satisfaction of a win to all. Mordialloc had contained a team ranked second only to Frankston in experience. And Mornington had overcome the strains of travel to finish the game without being overrun.

All players shook hands. The next thirty minutes were spent in conversation and toasting. Some players drank water. Charlie Allchin, for instance, would not have dared come home that night with the perfume of liquor on his breath, his mother being a founding member of the Mornington Abstinence Society. Hugh would have had what Charlie was having, water or lemonade. The other Caldwells were more likely to have had a glass of beer, rum or whiskey – though they were not boozers. Nowhere in the family writings does it say the brothers were anything other than prolific tea drinkers. The newspapers would later state there were up to ten teetotallers on the team. That left at least another ten who might have had a tipple of something with more kick.

It would not be credible to maintain that footballers, even those of impeccable character, didn't have an alcoholic beverage straight after games. Most footballers, until the recent rash of 'professionalism' and health consciousness, had ales or spirits within minutes of a match for a century and a half. It was cultural across all levels and still is in minor leagues.

In 1892 liquor merchants were so aware of drinking among footballers, they were already using images of the athletes for marketing. A newspaper advertisement on the same weekend of the Mornington-Mordialloc game ran in the major mastheads in Melbourne, promoting a multiple-prize-winning brand of whiskey called Galley, imported from the Scottish Highlands. The ad featured a drawing of three footballers – in knickerbockers and jerseys – standing on a boat with oars and a mast, each man holding a bottle of grog as big as his head. The boast from the merchant was: 'FOOTBALLERS PREFER GALLEY WHISKEY: EXCELS ALL OTHERS'. Behind the players, the sun was going down, as it was in Mordialloc within minutes of the drawn contest.

No one noticed any drunkenness as the players dressed warmly for the homeward journey. Hooper took the final sips of his lemonade and sarsaparilla and went to help his son and Coomber prepare the *Process*.

Thomas Rennison later recalled, 'One or two of the boys came up and shook hands with me.'

'I don't know you quite,' he said to the players. 'It's fifteen years now that I have been away from your place, but I knew all your people, for I was living there [The Point] forty years.'

He would later say, 'I never saw such a fine lot, the pride of the district.' The crowd dispersed quickly: locals walked home; visitors went to the train station. The wind had strengthened and was now whipping across the bay with a sharpness that chilled sun-softened skin. Darkness was changing from pink to purple the few clouds above the horizon; soon they would become shades of grey. The sun was diving fast.

'Come on, you fellows, hurry up!'

The urgings came once again from restless bank-man Henry Short, demanding his teammates stop lingering and head for the pier. Eventually, they did as he said. Four fishermen from Mordialloc came over to say goodbye. They knew Hooper well and were asking him to come back for a visit soon. One of them was Charles Droop. Another was named Charles Henwood. The players began stepping down into the *Process*. Lawrence, Caldwells, the Grovers . . .

Henwood, the Mordialloc fisherman, later recalled of that minute, 'I saw no drink in the boat and all in the boat were perfectly sober.' He did not think the vessel had too many people aboard it, though he added, 'With rough weather, I would say, with the large sail Hooper had on, it would be too many . . .'

Charlie Allchin was standing on the pier to say goodbye to his friends. Hooper had explained he could not take any more than he had brought to Mordialloc.

Then came some last-minute jockeying. Short was still hollering for the last men to move with greater speed. He looked frustrated and anxious.

Tom Coxhell was stalling. Still a bit sickly from the trip to the game, he didn't want to go back by sail. But he must have been having a hard time working up the courage to say so. He was hungry, tired and knew his wife and baby daughter would be waiting up for him. He just wanted to get home as quickly as possible, without suffering more seasickness.

Also, he didn't like the look of the sea starting to chop up. Later he would concede he had felt a 'presentiment' of doom.

Willie Coles had arrived and placed his trunk below the thwart. Charles Hooper junior, John Coomber and the skipper Hooper made their final preparations to leave.

Beside the boat stood four players: Charlie, Short, Coxhell and a Scotsman whose name was George Milne, known to all as 'Jock'. Milne had apparently caught the train to the match. The popular thirty-six-year-old married father of four was disappointed he had missed the chance to sail to the game and was itching to go home via the bay.

Hooper started doing a head count. All of a sudden, Short said he didn't want to wait any longer. He announced he would go home by rail.

'Don't be a cocktail,' Hooper said. But Short had made his mind up. He told his employee, young accountant William Grover, to come by his house later and pick up the keys to the bank. The arrangements for the long weekend weren't clear to anyone else, only that Short wanted Grover to be able to open up when he wasn't there.

Charlie Allchin, standing in his pants, suspenders and overcoat, carrying a bag with his linen (bringing it home for his mother to wash), saw his opportunity. He told Short he could have his train ticket, good all the way to The Point. At first Short said no, encouraging Allchin to come with him and go straight home to see his parents. But at that moment Charlie wanted nothing more than to sail in the *Process* with Hugh and the other Caldwells. He reached into his pocket, which contained a purse with a little more than one pound, his office keys and a train ticket. He handed the ticket to Short and took his place in the boat beside his mates.

Coxhell then followed the bank-man's lead and declared he was catching the train. He did not mention his fears before abruptly walking in the direction of the railway platform.

'Jock' Milne smiled and took Coxhell's place on the *Process*. When Hooper finished his count he realised he was one short of the party he had brought to Mordialloc. The man named P. Schultz had already gone for the station. Fifteen was his tally.

Many hands pushed the craft from the pier. By now the sea had become uneven. The wind was shifting further north. Hooper called to his crew, 'Give her a little board.' The board – or centreplate – would help keep them steady. Coomber lowered it to its full six feet and then helped the captain's son raise the sails. Hooper pointed the *Process* into the breeze and then turned her.

'Bearing away . . .'

There would be no tacking on the way home and they expected to arrive back at Mornington between eight and nine o'clock.

One of the fishermen who watched them depart would later say, 'They were a lot of really fine young men, who looked as if no serious harm in the world could come to them, ready to go anywhere and tackle anything.'

Forty-one

Minute by minute the bay was becoming slightly more challenging. Hooper had his crew trim the mainsails to limit their speed. According to another witness from the pier, the captain let out 'not an inch more sail than was safe'. Other sailors who were out on the bay that night later described conditions as 'lumpy'.

Captain Jack Bunn, of the Allchin family's *Maggie*, was sailing with stores from the city at about the same time the Mornington football team headed for a straight dash across the eastern edge of Port Phillip. His presence on the water confirmed it was not too dangerous to travel. If it had been too wild, he would have reluctantly stayed the night in the metropolis. He later told someone that 'the night was clear enough to see the land from nine miles out'.

Soon the players, sitting on the weatherside rail, would be close enough to Mornington to see the harbour's two lights: one on the pier and the other atop the highest bluff – Lighthouse Hill.

As the *Process* moved south along the coast, rising and falling over all-direction waves, delicate forces were now being balanced. The wind was pushing against the broad backs of the football teammates, whose weight was keeping the boat from tipping too far forward. The sail was taking all the wind it could. The wire stay, attached to the hull at one end and mast at the other, was holding firm. However, Hooper had experienced difficulties with the stay in the 'lumpy' weather at the regatta the year before.

If the captain, crew and players were fearful it was not showing. The youngsters in the party suggested some music. Coles played his cornet. Despite their fatigue, the footballers were loud enough to be heard from the shoreline as the *Process* passed Frankston, more than halfway home. By now the sky and bay were black but it mattered not. The carefree young men were singing only to each other. They could have been a thousand nautical miles from anywhere.

For some of the players, the elation of being together would have been the finest thing they had experienced in sport. Replaying the small incidents – brutal collisions and moments of skilfulness – from the previous few hours is one of the joys of football. To do it on a fast-moving yacht at night while being sprayed by salt water and singing in concert with dear friends and loved ones would have been the thrill of their young lives.

Forty-two

The train hauling jolly but weary football supporters from Mordialloc arrived at The Point after dark; its steam and the whistle were heard throughout the village. The Mornington football team's captain, Tom Coxhell, did not hang around the station. His was a three-minute walk home. He took it at once and was greeted by his wife, Eleanor, and daughter, Cecilia. He had been pondering all the way home whether he had made the right decision to split from those aboard the *Process*.

That decision saved his life. On arriving at his house, he had something to eat and went to bed. He slept soundly and went on to live another sixty-eight years. He would die in his Melbourne home aged ninety-two.

Henry Short arrived on the same train as Coxhell but did not go home. Instead, he walked with one of his other team-mates, fisherman Tom Hutchins, to the harbour to await the rest of the team. The pier was cold, almost freezing. It was as if winter had arrived while they were riding the train. The bay was now rolling and swaying and spitting.

Short and Hutchins, standing in the glow of the pier lamp's flame, supposed the *Process* was about a mile from land, its passengers coming closer to the coast with every passing second on a direct course to Mornington.

The wind was now coming straight from the northwest, as if ordered by Hooper. If nothing went wrong, they would soon be safely in port.

Forty-three

Just then a squall hit the harbour and almost blew Short and Hutchins over.

Squalls are common to Port Phillip. They usually arrive with cooling, changing winds, often as a new weather pattern pushes up the middle of the bay from Bass Strait. Sometimes they come with rain or a thunderstorm but not always. Big squalls can be seen looming from the west. Scrunching clouds and curtains of mist give them away. But at night, they are silent stalkers, unpredictable and dangerous.

Captain Jack Bunn, of the *Maggie*, would later report he felt several squalls on the bay that evening. One of them hit his vessel a second or two after an uncommon weakening of the northwesterly; it was so severe he had to 'shorten sail'.

The same wind burst, or another one just as strong, hit the *Process* as she approached The Point, though it is not precisely known how close the boat was to its destination.

Only Hooper, his son and their other crewman, Coomber, would have known what was happening when the wind went mad, particularly if it followed the same momentary lull Captain Bunn had witnessed, though Hugh and Charlie, the next most experienced in boats, may have guessed it was part of a severe squall. But there was nothing any of them could do about it.

The passengers on the rail – a majority of the team – who had been leaning into the wind as ballast, would have been thrown further backward with a sudden loss of force, as the sails came 'hard back on the mast'. Those who did not fall into the water would have tried to lurch forward to correct their balance and save themselves. A heartbeat later, when the wind powered up again, this time with greater punch, it would have refilled the canvases with a thud.

No matter how the wind struck, the squall was too much for the *Process* to endure; the fine balance between her equipment and people had been lost. The violent gust created unbearable pressure at both ends of the wire halyard holding the mast and sails in place.

It snapped and the mast broke and everything collapsed. Hooper, his crew and the footballers were tossed into the black waves. The boat began sinking.

In days after the accident, sailors and reporters and anyone with any knowledge of the bay would give their opinions about what happened to the *Process* when that squall caused its chaos. Some took to dramatic description, declaring the sound of the mast cracking was like a Deringer pistol being fired. All agreed the players' struggle for survival must have been 'sheer terror'.

Someone later said they heard – or did they? – the faint sound of Willie Coles' cornet being played in that fatal hour.

Tom Hutchins and Henry Short, who felt the mighty squall while standing on the pier, heard nothing but the wind itself. With the insight of a man trained to know the sea's strangest movement and outbursts, Hutchins said to Short, 'If the boys caught that they will receive a shake.'

So began Mornington's longest night.

IV

Scratches on the Hull

Forty-four

It was 9 pm. Main Street was quiet. Only the hotels were open. The town smelled of burning logs and chimney smoke. No one was yet panicking.

The *Wanderer* and a few smaller boats were rocking from side to side in the harbour. Short and Hutchins were still on the pier, waiting. No other family and friends of the footballers had joined them. Some assumed their loved ones had either stayed behind in Mordialloc for the night or had gone by train to Melbourne for a look at the 'theatre'.

Short was the first to become anxious. He could not stand in one spot any longer so he went up Main Street to poke around. At one of the pubs, he spoke to people, who 'expressed wonder how it was the party had not returned'. He was starting to hope the boat had turned back and landed at Mordialloc. That way the boys might have been able to borrow or hire a carriage to make it home by road. Maybe they were already back at The Point and he had not noticed.

It was an unlikely but more comforting theory. Short went home to see if young William Grover had called to drop in the bank keys. Nothing. Then he went down to the pier one more time. Hutchins, hands in his pockets, shook his head. It was time to call for help.

Short strode back up Main Street, past the police station, post office and Coffee Palace to his good mate J. D. Grover's place. Grover had been at the match earlier as a barracker; he had gone straight home after returning from Mordialloc on the same train as Short and Coxhell. Short's appearance on his doorstep was unsettling. When he was told about the no-show, Grover, whose son and brother were aboard the *Process*, dressed and went with the bank-man back down to the pier. At ten o'clock the wind worsened and the bay became mean. Waves began slapping the rocks on the headland, causing them to splash and drift over the pier and jetty.

Short, Hutchins and Grover spent the next hour trying to ignore their creeping angst. Hope soared when the men saw sails and a bow coming toward them. But it was Jack Bunn in the *Maggie*. He could tell them about the squalls but nothing more. He had not seen the *Process*.

Eleven o'clock.

There were people now emerging from their homes. Word had passed around that Hooper's boat was not in the harbour. Among the wonderers, if not yet fearful, was Charlie's mother, Sarah: standing by candlelight atop the Allchin's brick tower.

J. D. Grover was sick of waiting so he went back to his house and rigged a horse and buggy. Within minutes he was headed to Mordialloc at a hurried clip.

At 3 am, six hours after the boat was deemed late, Hutchins

and Short ended their vigil and went to their homes to escape the cold. They slept not a wink.

At the Presbyterian manse, Rev. Caldwell was awake, too. He had checked the breakfast room several times to see if his boys had made it home. He went there again to see if they had snuck in and were making themselves toast and tea. He found Alice sitting before a limp fire. Father and daughter read the dread on each other's face. Alice thought her papa looked unusually frail.

Rev. Caldwell dressed in his warmest coat and left the house before heading to the police residence to wake Senior Constable Thomas Murphy. In a broken voice the minister told the blue-eyed officer the *Process* was not yet back in Mornington. It might be lost on the bay.

'My three sons are with the party.'

From that moment Senior Constable Murphy was in charge of finding Jim, Willie, Hugh and the rest of the team. He was used to handling crises. As a young constable in Melbourne, Murphy had famously found the dead body of football's leading man Tom Wills after the sportsman stabbed himself with scissors. A subsequent promotion and posting to The Point gave the new senior constable and father of five a chance to be a community leader, a role he had relished until his family suffered a tragedy. Mornington's entire community had mourned for Senior Constable Murphy in 1891 when one of his children let go of a perambulator carrying his youngest baby, Stanley, who rolled down the cliffs and died.

No man in Mornington had confronted more grief – professionally and personally – than the local cop, who reached for his overcoat and hat before heading into the night air with the distressed clergyman.

Forty-five

Senior Constable Murphy and Rev. Caldwell rushed to the home of the postmistress and asked her to contact on the telegraph her colleagues in Mordialloc, or even Frankston, to find out whether the boat had docked in either town.

None of the many wire messages that went out over the next few hours were answered. The telegraph services did not operate twenty-four hours a day. The officer and minister discussed sending a search party of boats to look on the bay. But this idea was dismissed. They did not want to endanger anyone else. They would wait until the sun rose.

Concerned residents continued emerging from their houses and there was more activity in the village between 3 am and 4 am than on any other night in The Point's settlement. Sarah and Thomas Allchin were not among the dismayed; they had gone to bed. Sarah had decided Charlie was old enough to take care of himself. He had probably returned to Melbourne for some special long-weekend event, she thought, and the rest of the team could be anywhere.

But others were wandering up and down Main Street trying to find out what was happening. Alice Caldwell, still suffering from her cold, made her way at some point to the centre of town. Later, she would recall:

> No sooner was the news of the accident made known, and their names counted over, than it burst from the lips of people, among whom most of them had been born and bred, 'The cream, the very cream of Mornington is lost; the pick of the whole district was in that boat.'

Henry Short was still awake. How could he sleep? He went back to the pier. The wind had softened and become a south-westerly but was still ruffling the bay.

As he stood watching the harbour, which had nothing else to report, Short started talking to an older Mornington resident, Alexander McLellan, who had lived in the district for almost forty years. McLellan and his family were well known as the only Mornington family who had arrived in Australia aboard the infamous, diseased ship *Ticonderoga* in 1852. His sisters had gone to work at the Briars for Alexander Balcombe. Perhaps few people in the colony knew maritime horror the way Alexander McLellan recalled it. He was loosely related by marriage to James Firth, one of the boys on the *Process*.

It was about 5 am when Short and McLellan decided to find a carriage to take them to Mordialloc. Maybe the boat was anchored at Frankston. Maybe the team had taken refuge in the mouth of the man-made river that had been built to drain the Carrum Carrum swamp. Or perhaps the players had returned to their departure town and were taken in by Rennison for the night.

They were willing each other to think optimistically.

Senior Constable Murphy and Rev. Caldwell saw Short and McLellan leaving town and wished them luck. Another long-time resident of The Point, Cr William Irvine, was standing nearby. In an attempt to assuage the anxiety in Rev. Caldwell, he said, 'There's not a man or boy who comes into this place who can swim or dive better than your Hughie.'

Others were thinking the same. Among the majority of residents, speculation had been shifting from the team's whereabouts to who might be able to survive an awful accident.

Eyes were constantly veering from the water to the hills. Dawn was coming too slowly. It was soon realised nobody had heard from J. D. Grover.

By this time, Grover had arrived at Mordialloc on his buggy. He had searched the pier, beaches and creek. The *Process* was not there. He had roused Rennison, who said the last time he'd seen Hooper and the men was when they had sailed away after the match.

Feeling sick with worry, Grover had watered his horse and was heading back to Mornington, when he came across Short and McLellan going in the opposite direction. Each man read the other's expression and fell completely into despair. They had all but confirmed the boat was still on the water, if not under it. By the time they arrived back in Mornington, the town was lit from the faint glow of earliest sunrays. There was activity on the pier. Senior Constable Murphy was organising a search crew of fishermen.

Joseph Worrell, the former school, later wrote about the stress of waiting. He was most concerned for his dear friends Sarah and Thomas Allchin, whose son Charlie had not long ago sat beside him on a train ride to Melbourne, Worrell thinking all the way, 'what a fine man he was making'. He had taught most of the younger players on the football team, including Willie Coles, who he thought 'had turned out such a fine fellow', William Grover, who had a wife and child at home and was 'so comfortably settled', and the other William Grover, son of J. D., who was so big and strong. Worrell said it made his 'heart bleed' to see J. D. Grover and Rev. Caldwell at the pier that morning, as the fishermen rushed to set sail.

The flame on Lighthouse Hill had been refuelled and was reflecting on the bay's surface, which was now much calmer than before. The dawn brought flecks of brightness; there were pink streaks in the sky and blue ripples on the bay. The bluffs were glowing red but not for long. Clouds came to smother the eastern horizon and a wide shawl of fog fell fast over the peninsula and everything was at once without colour.

Three boats crawled north under sail. One of them was the *Progress*, skippered by Charles Hooper's brother. Senior Constable Murphy, who remained on land, had asked Fred Hooper to stay as close to the shoreline as possible while searching for his brother, nephew and the rest of the boys. The other vessels were to go a little further into the bay. By now a crowd had gathered on the pier and people stood spread out along rocks and sand and tree stumps. The football team captain Tom Coxhell was among them. He would later give an official statement to a coronial inquest.

> It was not until Sunday morning that I heard that the boat had not arrived. I immediately proceeded to the pier and that serious fears were entertained was evident from the fact that three fishing boats had departed to sea for the absent ones. From the pier and the surrounding hills and elevated points people anxiously gazed seawards.

All aboard the *Wanderer* had woken and were having something to eat when one of them saw the fishing boats pass. Henry Fergie called out to them and, on learning of their grave assignment, rushed his fellow sailors to lift the anchor. His logbook would later read:

> While at breakfast news came on board that a fishing boat containing fifteen persons had left Mordialloc the previous evening and that no news had been heard of them. It was at once decided to get underweigh [sic] and go in search of the missing boat Process.

Fergie's trusted sailing mate Arthur Peck picked up the marine glasses and climbed with them in his hand up to the crosstrees and peered northward.

Had Peck turned just a little to the starboard side – to gaze up at the clifftops – he would have seen Sarah Allchin standing once again on her mansion's brick tower. By now she had learned that Charlie was on the lost yawl. From her vantage, she had been watching the heartbreaking search get underway. Now she witnessed the *Wanderer* picking up speed.

Peck was shouting. *They've found something . . . make fast for it.*

Forty-six

The Presbyterian congregation sat motionless inside the church, looking up at Rev. Caldwell, who had chosen not to stay at the pier to watch the *Wanderer* tow the wrecked *Process* home; the parishioners waited for their revered minister to speak.

It was torturous for him to stand before them. But he did it because he was a man of service and discipline.

He began to read the sermon he had written while his sons were off playing football. But his moist eyes could not focus on the words. He was too shocked and saddened. He began crying.

There were other parents of the lost players in the church and they were looking at Rev. Caldwell now for some promise of hope, if not a miracle. Rarely, if ever, had the clergyman failed to deliver the message his worshippers needed. But he could not lie to them.

The Melbourne press would later report, 'The officiating minister, Mr Caldwell, broke down in the middle of his prayers, and was compelled to beg the indulgence of the congregation.'

After the service abruptly finished, the congregation followed Rev. Caldwell back down to the pier, where hundreds of people had gathered. The service of another church – St Peter's – had also ended prematurely. The Uniting Church minister, Reverend Benjamin Newport White, consoled his friend and fellow Irishman Rev. Caldwell, who then walked to the coastline where he stayed for a very long time; he cancelled his evening church service and was last seen that day walking with heavy boots along the beach.

Rev. White's daughter Celeste remembered until her dying days the moment she saw the town in mourning. Eighty years later she wrote in her diary, 'My mother and I heard the news coming out of the church and I looked toward the red bluff where there were little groups waiting – watching. The boat, overturned, was found with one body.'

Forty-seven

The naked body of Alfred Lawrence had been brought to shore. The *Wanderer*, *Process* and fishing boats used in the search were all tied up.

There was howling on the pier. A single voice had called out to Fergie and Peck as the *Wanderer* neared the jetty.

'Are they all dead?'

Silence was the grim answer.

Senior Constable Murphy was the first to identify young Lawrence, still in the craft that had carried him back to the harbour; the policeman had been searching the crowd for Alfred's father, Alfred Lawrence senior, the storekeeper. The Englishman and his wife, Ann, had nine children (a tenth had died in infancy) between the ages of five and twenty-one. They were known as generous and loving people.

'Have they found any bodies?' Lawrence senior asked the policeman in his withered British accent.

'They found your son.'

Lawrence took a second to understand those three words and he looked at the remorseless sky.

'Tell them to send him home,' he said. 'Tell them to send him home.' He then strode up Main Street without looking back.

Families inched forward to see the battered *Process*. Some of the footballers' clothes were still in her and onlookers identified them as belonging to their sons and nephews and brothers. Those who did not find their relatives' garments wondered whether some of the footballers had been able to swim to safety. Maybe some of young men were still sitting on a beach or marching through foreshore scrub on their way back to The Point. The wreck had been found *so close* to land. Why did they take off their clothes? How long were they in the water?

A mail carriage was used to carry Alfred Lawrence junior's body to his parents' shop, where several men 'laid their sorrowful burden'.

By now Senior Constable Murphy had wired the water police to request the government's steamer – *Lady Loch* – come down and drag the reef for victims. He had organised several land search parties. Men on drays, foot and horseback made their way to the point nearest the wreck site, off Mount Eliza. The first to arrive found two military overcoats. They belonged to Willie Coles and James Firth. But no bodies had washed up. News of the accident was soon spreading across the country. Journalists arrived in Mornington from Melbourne on the same day. A special Sunday evening edition of the *Herald* was published. Senior Constable Murphy made a public statement:

> Of course the search will be continued both ashore and afloat until all hope of finding any more bodies is past. There is little probability that any of the party could have reached the shore alive.

An inquiry was held the next day into the death of Alfred Lawrence at his parents' store in Main Street. Henry Fergie, who was a Justice of the Peace, stayed in the town to act as magistrate. He found, 'Alfred Lawrence came by his death through drowning when returning with a football party in the fishing smack *Process* from Mordialloc to Mornington on the night of the twenty-first day of May 1892.'

The end was simple but the inquest was as thorough as possible. Senior Constable Murphy gave evidence, stating he had known Lawrence for two-and-a-half years.

'He was a quiet well conducted young man whom I had never known to touch a glass of drink,' the policeman told the inquiry.

Alfred Lawrence senior gave brief evidence, identifying the body and stating his son was nineteen years and two months.

Charles Henwood, the fisherman who had said farewell to the party at Mordialloc, was called to say what he saw and to give his views on the weather. Arthur Peck gave evidence on finding the wreck and recovering the body. The next day a large cortege walked from Main Street to the outskirts of Mornington, to see Alfred Lawrence buried. It was the largest funeral march the district had seen; several hundred people walked in front of no fewer than fifty carts and carriages and thirty horsemen. Leading the procession was Tom Coxhell, Henry Short, the Rovers, and all football club supporters. Wreaths and 'emblems' were placed on the coffin. And men, women and children of The Point held hands and wept as the youth was lowered into the sandy earth.

Forty-eight

Rev. Caldwell sent a telegram to his son Tom in Tasmania, saying Jim, Willie and Hugh were 'lost in the bay on Saturday night'. Tom had not yet read the note when one of his neighbours arrived at his front gate.

'Have you seen the paper?' said the neighbour solemnly.

'Not yet.'

It was Tom's habit to send a farm hand in a horse and cart to the town of Dunorlan for stores, post and a newspaper. He had been waiting for them to be brought to him.

'Oh, Tom,' said the neighbour. 'I don't want you to see the paper.'

The neighbour had been to Dunorlan earlier and seen a group of people gathered outside the post office reading the headlines and details of the calamity. The postmistress had asked him to 'take a message to Mr Caldwell'.

'The truth is there is dreadful news for you. Something terrible, in fact. Here is the telegram.'

Alice Caldwell would later write of this moment:

> Tom took the telegram with that calmness that comes to us in the supreme moments of our life, and before breaking the seal, Jim's face rose before him, just as he had seen it last, with the strangely unfathomable look in the mystic eyes, just as they had looked at him, as he and Tom stood together for the last time on earth on the little railway station in Westbury.

'It is dreadful, dreadful,' said the neighbour. 'A whole boatful lost, and not one living to tell the tale. I don't believe I could ever bear such a blow.'

From the telegram, Tom knew only that his brothers had died. He assumed they had foundered in Hugh and Charlie's homemade boat.

'What?' he said. 'You don't mean to tell me there are more than three boys lost?'

'Yes, there were a lot of them coming from a football match at some place or another, and a squall struck the boat and not one of them was saved.'

'Now, I understand,' said Tom.

Tom decided to go to Mornington and search the shore with his father. But before leaving he received one more piece of mail. It was a letter written by Willie the day before the accident, thanking Tom again for the lovely time he had last summer. Willie had written that he would like to visit again next summer.

Back in Mornington, Rev. Caldwell was a central figure of grief.

'I would have died for those boys,' he said one day to Alice while sitting among the ti-tree.

'I am sure you would, Papa,' Alice said. 'I would have died for any of them, but for the three I would have been torn to pieces.'

Thomas Allchin wasn't as physically fit as Rev. Caldwell and stayed close to his property, awaiting news of the search for bodies, which was seen as more and more hopeless after the *Lady Loch* came with the wrong equipment and went back to Melbourne. Looking at the bay from his front yard, Thomas saw the Presbyterian minister one day and comforted him. They watched a gardener pass them by.

'There goes the man to prune the trees and there will be no Charlie and Hughie to eat the fruit this year,' said Charlie's father. 'They used to eat as much as they wanted here and then go down to your place and have another lot there. Poor boys, poor boys.' He could not hold back his tears after that.

The Allchins and Caldwells spent the days after the accident together. Charlie's mother, Sarah, was a loving friend to Alice Caldwell. The women had long talks.

'Though the manner of their death was terrible, too terrible to even let our thoughts dwell on it,' Alice said to Sarah one night. 'If possible, still their memories are very sweet and pleasant. I sit for hours thinking of them. In fact, they are never out of my thoughts, night and day, and it is a great thing to be able to look away from the dark picture of their deaths to that of their bright and happy lives.'

Sarah said, 'Yes, I have not a memory of Charlie that is not pleasant.'

Still, they ached for their lost relatives' bodies to be found so they could be given a proper Christian burial.

Visitors came to town and expressed feelings of the tragedy and loss. The Scotch College principal, Dr Morrison, came to the Caldwell house and assured Rev. Caldwell, 'He shall keep them in the grave that He has prepared for them.'

Charlie's well-known architect boss, Alfred Dunn, arrived on the Tuesday after the accident. Mr Dunn said he couldn't believe what had happened and that they were all gone. And he was not alone. Though the truth had to be accepted, it was still too hard to comprehend that a boat found so close to the shore could not offer some survivors.

Slow believers used as reasons for their incredulity the example of the *Loch Ard*, which came from England and crashed on the 'Shipwreck Coast' (west of The Heads) in 1878. The captain, named Gibb, was disoriented by the fog and came too close to the rocks. By the time he realised where he had sailed, the ocean swell was his master, throwing the three-masted ship backwards onto the reef. Lifeboats went down with the ship within ten minutes. Some died from the crash but others were left thrashing in the water.

There were two survivors: Eva Carmichael and Thomas Pearce. Eva held onto a spar for five hours in the freezing sea; Thomas made it to shore and went back to save her when he heard her shouts for help.

Five hours in colder water than Port Phillip . . .

Forty-nine

While the searchers were still trawling the water's edge for bodies and answers, J. D. Grover told people he was certain his brother and son had died but 'for Hughie, he hoped for the last'. Hugh Caldwell, he thought, could 'keep himself afloat in almost any sea'.

For 124 years this question of survival has clung like a barnacle to the story of the *Process*. To find the answer, there must be another secret revealed – where the accident actually happened, because it was not at the point it was later found floating.

Some have speculated that the ship tacked its way to Mornington and could have found itself as far west as three miles from the coast. But there were no significant changes of direction. The wind from the northwest made sure there were only two courses the *Process* could have taken: one was a straight line from Mordialloc to Mornington; the other was from Mordialloc deeper into the bay with one tack, before making a beeline to The Point.

Either way, it would not have made much difference. By the time Hooper had nearly arrived at Mornington, the boat was either a mile from shore or a little further. Taking into account the statements about weather and visibility from Captain Bunn, of the *Maggie*, it is certain the team would have been able to see Lighthouse Hill and Mornington pier. They may even have been able to see the outline of the *Wanderer*.

In only one newspaper report, hidden among thousands of words, is a reference to a barrel of oil being anchored in the bay – a suggestion it may have been an unignited distress signal. It was apparently a mile out. This was not mentioned in any subsequent inquiry. Maybe it wasn't true or maybe it didn't matter to the investigators who were more interested in finding out about the involvement of liquor, overloading or the seaworthiness of the *Process*.

In all the documented evidence, there seems a lack of interest in the precise location of the accident. Perhaps, at the time, it wasn't important that it happened here and not over there. If the barrel of oil were there, it would surely have marked the spot.

There would be more evidence revealed to suggest the players were at least a mile away from the land. But that would be found later.

A mile. Just over fifteen hundred metres. An Olympic swimmer would do that in about fifteen minutes. An amateur who had grown up diving for hammers and anchor chains in the bay might take twenty. With an onshore breeze it would be a faster swim. The wind's origin, at some point very late that night, moved from the northwest to the southwest, Port Phillip's uniform breeze. It was suddenly coming from the bay's most southern reaches and pushing the broken *Process* to a spot between Mornington and Frankston.

What were the chances players stayed alive clutching to the *Process* for one, two, three, four or five hours? First, it is wiser to ask: what were the chances they lasted five minutes in the water before drowning?

Unlike people on a passenger ship, the players had punished their bodies that day. Short of running a marathon, a game of football is the most draining activity a young man can complete. It is also harder to play four quarters early in the season because your body is not conditioned to it. The Mornington players had not played many games since 1891 and would have been suffering fatigue within the first quarter.

Football is a different experience for players all over the country. In the north, Darwin or the Tiwi Islands, the heat invades your body and humidity feels like it's cooking you from the inside. Furthest south, in Hobart, the game is easier to play; the cooler air might freeze your toes and fingers for a while but you can warm up with long socks and longer runs. In Queensland, the heat is nothing to worry about. The winter sun *slowly* warms you and bathes you in wonderful, cleansing sweat. In Victoria the season is long enough to boil you in April and chill you from June. May and September are the moderate times, although a lack of conditioning can cause cramping in the earliest games.

The sport strains every muscle. Toward the end of the match the Mornington players would have been enduring something modern coaches call 'high neural fatigue'. Each action – a chase of the freed ball, a spring in the air, a lunge to tackle, a wrestle, a punch – was causing their brains to constantly give messages to their muscles. This was making them puff and suck air and feel faint from the effort, symptoms of a weakening neural system. To recover from this completely, they needed to sleep.

Their muscles were without doubt tearing all afternoon, though not necessarily causing pain. 'High intensity muscle contractions' cause microfibres to wear and stretch just a bit each time. At the end of the game the players would have felt most tired in their legs, chests and forearms. For an accumulation of stresses, add to this general soreness the inevitable knocks that cause acutely felt injuries: corked thighs, gashed flesh, a snapped finger, busted nose, sprained ankle, or ripped-off toenails.

None of this was a problem before the cowbell rang. Adrenaline numbs the pain, until the game is over. Then the body replays the blows for the mind. And the slow physical recovery begins.

Walking back to the boat, the players would have been between one and three per cent lighter from dehydration – limbs stiffening by the minute. Those who had a nip or two of liquor would have been the first to start falling into a lovely state of drowsiness. By the time the players were hit by a squall a mile or so from shore they would have been still, relaxed and caked with salt from sweat and spray.

Then came the plunge.

Those who survived the accident and could make it past or through the fallen rigging to hold onto the boat had another challenge to overcome as their environment went from air to water. Cold shock.

The risk of being killed by the water's temperature had been recognised long before the Mornington team was slung into Port Phillip during winter's onset in 1892. Herodotus wrote in 450 BC about deaths at sea in the Persian battle fleet against Athens, 'Those who could not swim perished from that cause, others from the cold.' In countless nineteenth-century maritime disasters people lived beyond the accident to die in the water, awaiting rescue.

The range of survival times varies from minutes to hours, depending on the survivor.

Plunge into the bay as the Mornington team did on that frigid night and you will suffer four basic stages of capitulation. During the first three minutes your skin will cool; during the next twenty-five minutes your muscles slowly seize and freeze; then the cold will spread to your organs; and then, sometime after that, hypothermia will start to alter your body *and* mind. Hypothermia, the last stage of breakdown in people trapped in cold water, does not kill nearly as many people as the effects of the first two stages.

With the temperature of the water at about ten or eleven degrees, the immersed players would have first lost their breath and gasped for more air, swallowing water by hyperventilating and thrashing about. The 'vasoconstriction' of blood cells would have forced their hearts to beat as fast as possible. Fear may have worsened both reactions, which would have lasted up to three minutes. A heart attack can kill someone in those same circumstances but is unlikely in fit young men.

Hyperventilating people become confused. Deep inhaling can seem like suffocation. People who can hold their breath for a minute on land can hold it for just ten seconds in cold water. Gasping with their mouths only slightly above the surface of a 'lumpy' bay, players would most likely have involuntarily consumed a lot of seawater. It is almost certain some of the out-of-breath footballers drowned within a minute of the accident.

But most would have survived, at least for a little while. Their bodies would have recovered from the shock. Then they would have grabbed the boat, the broken mainmast, the mizzenmast, the centreboard, the rail, or anything that floated. And one by one they took their clothes off.

The safest thing for them to do was to take off heavy coats and boots, anything that prevented them paddling about. They almost all did this. The next best way to keep shielded from the cold was to leave the rest of their clothes on. But some went further. Lawrence took all his clothes off. Maybe he survived longer than the rest. It's possible he was not thinking clearly when he removed the last of his undergarments. Then he became entangled and trapped.

Stay in the water long enough and your skin will go numb. Then the coolness seeps into your muscles and joints. This is the beginning of paralysis. It starts with your hands and then goes to your forearms. Within five minutes your fingers will lose strength. The longer you are in the water, the more disabled you become. It is not about will or determination. It's as if your body is going to sleep with or without you knowing.

The players were increasingly desperate to climb out of the water, confirmed by the scratches on the hull. In time, they would have discussed whether to stay with the wreck or swim for shore. After surviving the cold shock and subsequent loss of strength, even Hugh might have struggled to get far from swimming. First, he probably would not have been able to breathe well enough to maintain a proper stroke. More gasping. No power. Numb fingers splayed. Shivering. Legs sinking. Even for the best swimmer in the world, a mile would seem like forever after about fifty yards.

It is likely that if one player swam for help no one would have followed. Instead, they stayed and watched in horror as each man – one after the other – disappeared from sight and never returned.

While this struggle went on and no search party was launched, the *Process* was drifting closer and closer to land.

Fifty

If this story had a hero it was Senior Constable Murphy, who led a tireless search for the bodies, despite the town – nicknamed 'Mourningtown' by some in the press – falling into a pit of sadness. People turn to a leader or leaders in a crisis. And someone, who is not necessarily stronger but more able to cope with carnage, steps forward and raises a hand to say, 'I will do it because it must be done.' Mornington's policeman led searches until the back of his eyes throbbed from lost sleep.

The Caldwell men were almost as tireless. For weeks Rev. Caldwell was spotted 'walking distractedly by the edge of the waves with his gaze turned seawards'.

Tom Caldwell arrived from Tasmania and wore a path along the coast with his father, whose face and beard grew whiter and longer by the day. Tom walked 'mile upon mile, and spent hour upon hour searching upon the lonely seashore for the bodies of his beloved dead'. It can be assumed he longed most painfully for Jim, his farming partner and housemate, because that's the brother he spoke about when he bumped into other searchers in the week following the accident.

'It is when you come to compare Jim with men of his own age,' he would say. 'That you can see what he was.'

He missed Jim's voice.

'Jim would talk sensibly on any subject,' Tom added. 'But most of the fellows that I meet with now can yarn away by the hour, and when they have done you can't remember a word of what they have talked about.'

His sister Alice also ached for Jim. Perhaps she saw him as the most vulnerable of her three lost siblings. Or maybe it was because she did not see him as often and wished they had spent more time together. An old friend of the family came to visit Rev. Caldwell, Alice, Tom and the little ones. She gave Alice her deepest sympathies. And they talked about 'the boys'.

'It is not right to have favourites in families, and I often fought against it,' Alice said to the family friend, an older lady called Mrs Grice.

'Ah, dear, we can't help it,' Mrs Grice said. 'Even a mother can't. And when one does everything in his power to make all around him bright and happy, we can't help loving that one the most. It is only natural.'

Jim Caldwell would never be found, though his coat was picked up from the shallow water south of Mornington, near Dromana, a week after the accident. Nothing else. Was he one of the first players to die? His family imagined so. He had been a good swimmer but was out of practice. As Tom told Alice, 'after sitting in the boat some time, he would have been too stiff for any great exertion'.

Alice later wrote, 'That the actual shock of being cast upon the sea would not kill him, I know; he was too robust in mind and body, and I have always prayed that none of those poor fellows were struck by the falling mast, so as to enter eternity without a moment's warning. He might have entered Parliament, where gentlemen and gentlemen's sons are too seldom to be met with. There was more sense and goodness in Jim's little finger than there is in the whole of the body of some of our members.'

His bones lie somewhere on the bay's bed, beside his brother Tom's watch and the locket he was given by his workmates in Melbourne, before he went to Eaglehawk and started living the best life he imagined.

Willie Caldwell also drowned with his watch, given to him by his 'Papa' after winning one of his scholarships at Scotch College. He had worn a 'macintosh' coat that was never found.

Hundreds upon hundreds of sympathetic telegrams arrived in Mornington before the end of May. They came from clubs, families, friends and community leaders. His Excellency the Governor of Victoria wrote, 'Lady Hopetoun and I desire to express deep sorrow at the catastrophe which occurred last Saturday night and beg you will convey our sincerest sympathy to the bereaved relatives of the victims of the accident.'

No player on the missing team was talked about as much in the telegrams as Willie Caldwell. On Monday morning a note addressed to Rev. Caldwell arrived from Ormond College's esteemed master, Dr MacFarland. It read, 'Accept the sincere sympathy of your son's fellow students in your terrible bereavement.'

Another telegram came on the same day – also addressed to Rev. Caldwell – from Willie's closest studying mate at university. Dave Officer wrote, 'It is difficult for me to find the words with which to express my intense grief and sorrow for you, in the appalling loss you have sustained by such an untimely accident. When I left Will last Friday, little did I think that such an awful event was in the near future. You have lost in him and his brothers good sons, and I have lost a dear companion and mate – one who was in the truest English sense, a man, and during our term as room mates . . . that friendship was never once ruffled by a single word. In the deep sorrow of yourself and family there is, however, some small consolation in the thought it must have been the will of God. With heartfelt sympathy and condolence in your great bereavement.'

One of the telegrams regarding Willie was not signed by name; rather by 'one of Willie's old school fellows'.

> You will wonder at who is the stranger to you intruding on your awful grief, but I knew and admired your dear son, Willie, and were it not that I have a deep sense of his worth and a deeper sense of his loss, I should not write this. I was at the Scotch College with him, and the University, and at both places the gracious, kindly qualities of his mind and heart made him beloved by all who knew him. 'Grief makes mothers of us all,' and my sadness makes me feel for you and yours, but my grief is tempered with the thought that he lived and died worthily. I, who have known and loved him, will ever

> cherish his memory, will ever remember the kindly smile that lit up his features, the right path that he trod, always with a kind word ready and a helping hand to lend the weak. Strong, trusty, true, and noble, the cold sea hath his body, but his soul lives on high, and we who have known him will never forget his kind and gracious manner.

There were notes from almost all the medical students in Melbourne and all the teachers who had Willie in their classes at Ormond and Scotch, which were said to be 'greatly depressed at his early death'.

Late in the week, Dr MacFarland wrote another note to his friend Rev. Caldwell. It was longer and more personal and would be treasured by the grieving minister.

It read, in part:

> Accept my heartfelt sympathy. The college is gloomy to-day. What must your home be? Willie was loved by all. He was a favourite of my own, and for your sake, as well as his, I took the greatest interest in his progress. He never cost me an anxious moment, and I looked forward to a bright future for him. I felt assured you would feel yourself repaid for any sacrifices you were making to give him a University career . . . No one but yourself and your family will miss Willie more than I do. I wish I could bear a little of the burden. As it is, I can only offer you my deepest sympathy . . .

The searching went on and one day someone found Willie Caldwell's bag on a peninsula beach. It had his football uniform in it.

For the next month, Senior Constable Murphy was still urging volunteers to keep looking for bodies. One burial was not enough.

There was also urgency in trying to care for those parents, wives, mothers and children left 'almost destitute' by the loss of their 'bread winners'. A public meeting was held on the Tuesday after the accident, chaired by the shire president and attended by all, including politicians from Melbourne.

The minutes expressed 'profound sympathy with all those who have lost relatives and friends in the recent disaster' and resolved to raise funds by making an 'earnest appeal to the public of Victoria for its general assistance'.

Joseph Worrell was made secretary of the Relief Committee and Henry Short became the treasurer. A subscription list was opened and those in the room kicked in 120 pounds, evidence of the outpouring of sorrow and generosity even during a Depression. A resolution was carried thanking Mr H. P. Fergie and the other yachtsman on the *Wanderer* for their 'prompt and valuable assistance after the accident'.

Fergie had been another impressive figure in the days after the tragedy. He had helped with the initial death inquest for the Lawrence family. This was done as quickly as possible so the body could be burned and remains buried. On the Wednesday, the people of Mornington wrote a letter to the yachtsman, finishing with the comment: 'Thank you for your kindness, in assisting as you did, you will never be forgotten by the people of this place.'

Fergie wrote back two days later from his office in Melbourne, revealing that he believed a night-time search party would have been able to save some of the footballers.

> Had authentic information as to the departure of the ill-fated boat from Mordialloc reached us earlier I have no doubt but that such assistance might have been rendered that probably a life or lives might have been saved and fewer left to mourn over such a terrible disaster.

Then he donated five pounds.

The regret of not searching earlier for the players began to weigh on everyone. A Marine Board inquiry was held and among the minutes scribbled in a dusty old book that remains in the Public Records Office in Melbourne today, there is evidence of one of the earliest discussions about boating safety in Port Phillip.

Inspectors for the Marine Board looked closely at the *Process*, examining its hull and rigging. For the first time an expert questioned whether the yacht was in perfect condition. In fact, the halyard – or wire stay – had been worn down and may have been susceptible to snapping under pressure even before Hooper took the team out.

The minutes read, 'Upon inspection of the gear . . . found that the main halyards (steel wire) 1¼ inches in circumference had carried away in the wake of the sheave hole at the masthead, they [Marine Board inspectors] carefully examined the strands where broken, and found that they showed that considerable chafe must have taken place previous to the carrying away, which would have been apparent to anyone upon examination.'

The board also said it was unwise for anyone to carry unsecured ballast, which surely made the *Process* boat sink from the stern. Had the ballast been secured and spread evenly, the players might have been able to stay in or climb back into the *Process*, even though it had taken on water.

The Marine Board did not criticise Hooper directly, stating: 'Charles Hooper was competent to sail a boat having followed the occupation of fisherman from boyhood.'

Among the conclusions was that if the telegraph station had been attended at Mordialloc, a search party would have been on the bay by midnight. The board suggested better communication should be made available 'all day and night'. Finally, it requested that its rules committee 'take this matter into consideration with a view of making such regulations as will tend to minimise such accidents as that which occurred at Mornington'.

But regulations do not save people from their mistakes. Before the inquiry was done, two fishermen from Frankston were lost in the bay. Their boat was found overturned and floating many miles from where they had last been seen. The fishermen were never seen again.

One of the people who gave evidence to the Marine Board in the case of the *Process* was Charles Hooper's brother. Fred Hooper and three other men would die five years later in Mornington harbour during a Fishermen's Race in the 1897 Easter Regatta.

It was a day of nasty weather. The sea was wild but organisers went ahead with the competition. Hooper's boat – *Progress* – foundered mid-race. The thirty-nine-year-old father of one drowned before a helping hand could grab him. His first mate, a man named William Allen, was rescued by another yacht. The only survivor from Hooper's boat gave an account of his struggle for life that gave all in

Mornington an idea of how the team might have thrashed about in 1892.

> The sea was worse than I ever remember. I said to Hooper that we were carrying too much sail, and he said that he agreed with me. I never saw such seas in all my life. They seemed to be climbing over us like mountains. Suddenly I saw a tremendous sea following us . . . There was nothing left of the boat but the tiller and I made for that, when I saw Hooper swimming towards me. I said to him. 'It isn't much, but it may help you. You'd better take it.' Then I struck out for the shore. We were all good swimmers. Then I swam for shore, where I could see spectators, but I found that the seas were so heavy that it was almost impossible to keep myself afloat. When I was almost exhausted I saw the *Helen* making toward me. So far as I could, for I was nearly exhausted, I raised myself above the wave, which almost suffocated me, and shouted. She went within four hundred yards of me and never saw me. About this time I saw one of the buoys marking the line of the race and swam towards it. The sea was so high it was almost impossible to hold on, but I saw that if I could fasten the rope holding the buoy from her mooring I might float on it to land. As the buoy rose I tried to loosen the rope with my teeth and fingers.

Eventually the *Helen* saved Allen. Another relief fund was set up for the Hooper family, mourning another lost father.

In the winter of 1892, tributes came from Melbourne for the Allchin family as they had for Willie Caldwell. Charlie's boss, Alfred Dunn, visited The Point more than once to give his regards to Sarah and Thomas Allchin. Dunn, who was only in his twenties, would die two years later from illness. Like Charlie, he never reached his potential as a man to help shape the future of a city enduring its harshest economic era.

Minutes from a meeting of Victoria's Architectural and Engineering Association said members 'spoke in feeling terms of high qualities and ability possessed by the deceased.'

Sarah and Thomas were comforted by the tributes to their son. Sarah wrote this letter to her other son, Tom, before he came from Queensland to join the search.

> My dear Tom,
> My heart is so sore and my eyes so heavy. I do not know if I can write yet but you must think the time long since the first telegram. It has been the longest week in my life, a week of suspense and anguish. The 9th day and not one of the 14 bodies found but I suppose you will have seen the daily telegram and up till dusk to night the steamer and boats have been dragging without success. We had hoped some would have floated yesterday and today but Saturday and Sunday were both very rough and windy and I fear any remains would be carried out through the night . . . We have received over fifty messages and telegrams, cards and letters of sympathy though I never go out or see anyone.
>
> My poor boy he will never come for me again. There appeared such a grand opening in the world for him. He knows best but it is a hard blow to humanity. Everyone loved Charlie. He had not an enemy. The last Monday morning he left, the 16th, I shall never forget his cheery 'Goodbye

> Mother, Goodbye Father' and off he went whistling to the station, never to return to me and not one left to tell the tale. They say that after the exciting football they would be so exhausted that they would not be able to swim as far in such piercing cold.

The Allchins knew that Charlie, who would have turned twenty the Saturday following the accident, did not die straight away. His trousers, with braces attached, were found in the *Process*, with his bag of linen nearby.

Nineteen days after the accident, the ranks of the search parties had thinned but their efforts continued. All along the coast they were checking the beaches every morning and evening for the footballers' remains. A carpenter from Frankston named John Engblom was walking near Mount Eliza when he saw a dead man lying face down on the sand, dressed in dark-blue tweed trousers, a blue serge vest over a red-and-white football guernsey and socks, no boots. The person looked to Engblom as if he had been 'thrown up by the sea'.

Senior Constable Murphy was alerted and came at once. The dead man's face was unrecognisable from decomposition, 'parts of the face being quite eaten away'. The officer and Engblom wheeled the corpse to the Mornington police station.

Murphy, not yet knowing who they had found, reached into one of the footballer's pockets and retrieved a leather purse holding four one-pound notes, a two-shilling piece and a penny. He also found sixpence in the bottom right-hand vest pocket. He then undressed the body.

Grieving relatives came to the station to see who had been found and they were shown the purse and clothing. A man named John Jenkins said he thought they belonged to his nephew and employee, James Firth. Jenkins then took the belongings to his wife, Helen, for a second opinion. Helen was the sister of James' father, John.

She had three brothers – John, James and William – all early settlers in Moorooduc near Mornington. She confirmed the clothing belonged to young James. The Scottish Firth clan had come to Australia from the Orkney Islands in the late 1840s and made a house of clay slabs. The brothers were renowned for being muscular and willing; they were among the first to log trees by hand – white, blue and peppermint gum – and transport them to the new Schnapper Point jetty so they could be taken to Melbourne. The bullock they used for dragging the timber doubled as makers of roads.

John Jenkins told Senior Constable Murphy at a death inquest later that day his nephew had, 'Never returned but is supposed to be drowned. I have seen the deceased but it is so decomposed that I cannot recognise it.'

James Firth, a member of the Victorian Rangers, the type of young man eulogised in Anzac Day ceremonies every year, was given the military funeral his family had wanted.

The same day Firth was found another corpse washed up at Rosebud, several miles south of Mornington; the high tide carried it in and left it on the beach. It was half a body, whose hands were held above its head and legs were missing. The fisherman who found it went to the local policeman, Mounted Constable William Norwood, who noted the body's dress: 'black vest, buttoned shirt, reddish check and flannel singlet, and brace' – no football gear. Maybe it wasn't one of the footballers, he thought. Mounted Constable Norwood sent a message to Senior Constable Murphy, who asked for the body to be brought to Mornington.

Another cart with a covered corpse rolled into Main Street. The people stood and watched. It was all they could do.

A man named Frederick Gowty came to Mornington Police Station later that day. He was a blacksmith from Geelong, who had moved to Mornington temporarily to live with Charles Hooper's widow. Gowty took a look at the half-body and thought it might be young Charles Hooper, the thirteen-year-old son of the *Process*' skipper. The relative took the black vest back to his sisters, who said it belonged to her son. All this happened on the late Charles Hooper junior's fourteenth birthday.

Five days after the discovery of the second and third bodies, an exhausted but determined Tom Caldwell was still scouring the coast. He did not want to go back to Tasmania without finding his brothers. Every morning he awoke in the family manse, ate a meal in the breakfast room, dressed for the cold, and set out to hike along the wind-shaped clifftops. Finally, he found a body, not far from where James Firth was washed up. It was wasted and had parts missing. Tom knew only that it wasn't Jim, Willie or Hugh. He didn't dare touch the remains and sent word of his find through a nearby resident to Senior Constable Murphy.

Another identification was needed. This time the body wore boots. The policeman showed the footwear to one of the local bootmakers, Thomas Hutchinson, who recognised the mark on the toe that he'd mentioned earlier to young John Kinna, the telegraph operator.

Kinna was laid to rest in the same dignified service held by the families of Lawrence, Firth and Hooper.

Still, Tom Caldwell – or the 'Boss', as his brothers once called him – kept wandering through his emotional wasteland, wanting to go home but unable to leave his task.

One day someone found found Willie Coles' trunk, then his cornet on the southern peninsula beaches. All were handed back to families, grateful for anything.

Back in Mornington the *Process* was being repaired. Charles Hooper's brother said he would put it to work. It would one day be passed to one of Charles' sons, George, who was seven when his father died. The *Process* would be used for fishing in Port Phillip for decades, long enough to have a motor installed. Within three years, Charles Hooper's wife, Maria, would marry another local fisherman and have more children.

Life insurance claims were paid quickly. George Milne's family received twenty-five pounds in a hurry. Apparently the man everyone called 'Jock' had only recently taken out a policy. His wife and children were now considered 'destitute', even with the payout.

During this awful time, people who knew the victims and those who did not know them wrote poems and songs. A football-song writer from Carlton, James Purtell, wrote a poem to aid the fundraising. In part it read:

And picture Mr Caldwell, too,
In wild and deep despair.
The loss of his three noble sons,
Is dreadful hard to bear.
O God it was a fearful blow,
And something truly sad,
Enough to break the stoutest heart,
And drive the strongest mad.

A final clue to the lasting mystery of the accident's location came with the discovery of a piece of clothing in faraway Sorrento. It was Hugh Caldwell's overcoat, with one sleeve half turned out. This remains the strongest evidence that the boat was as far as a mile out, but maybe even further, when it came to grief. The tide could not have floated his coat such a distance against the southwesterly if the squall struck the *Process* closer to the coastline. Hugh must have been one of the first to react by freeing himself of his heaviest clothing.

Alice wrote, 'I always feel that Hughie had a long struggle. If Hughie were free to have pulled off both his coats and he wore a heavy cloth overcoat which must have been thrown off first, Hughie would have lived long hours, and had boats only gone out that night it is probable at least one of our boys would have been saved.'

Sadness weighed upon the residents of the Caldwell house for a long time. Even Jim's new horse, the one he had broken in, was upset, unwilling to let anyone else handle her. Rev. Caldwell would have liked to have given the filly another home but couldn't do it.

'I never go out into the paddock and see that young horse, but I think of poor Jim,' he told Alice. 'He had her as quiet as a lamb. He was so kind and gentle with everything.'

Alice felt the same torment when she went into the bedroom Willie had slept in the night before the match. She always remembered Hugh talking to Willie on the Saturday.

'I say, Bill, you needn't take any money with you today,' Hugh said. 'I have enough for both of us.'

By spring, The Point was again flowering and no other bodies returned to land. Tom Caldwell went back to Tasmania. He said goodbye to his father, stepmother and his remaining four siblings. They hoped to visit him soon.

Little Jack was not so little anymore. He was twelve and growing like a weed. In summer, he asked to see Tom and was given his father's permission. He arrived at Eaglehawk and met old one-eyed Jock, who was kind and compassionate, as were his cousins and other locals. There seemed to be a flow of guests coming to see if Tom was okay. One of the visitors was a little boy, three or four years old, son of a nearby farmer. His mother brought him by to say hello.

After introductions, the mother said to her son, 'Who gave you rides? Tell Jack who gave you rides on his big horse.'

'Dim Caldwell,' said the cute boy.

'Yes, your brother used to always put him up on his horse when he came over to see us,' the mother told Jack, listening with intent. 'And he never forgets that.'

Jack and his sisters Jeannie and Sallie would grow up understanding their brothers were lovely men. Their big sister Alice would never let them forget it. She started writing their biographies. In her book *Love's Tribute* there can be found only one thought that gave her some comfort.

> Never, until that awful night, when you three boys met with such a terrible and untimely death, did I cease to regret that our mother had been taken from us so early in life. But when I realised the awfulness of the sorrow that had befallen us, I said, from the depths of my heart, 'Thank God, Mamma did not live to see this day.' It would have killed her.

Fifty-one

It was the *Argus* newspaper that published the line: 'Such an accident has no parallel in our land's history; similar cases may have occurred in other countries, but never in Australia.' It was true then and remains true today.

The Mornington tragedy claimed the lives of more than one per cent of the town's population; that statistic places it among the worst sporting-team accidents the world has witnessed, though somehow it has slipped from Australia's consciousness. Certainly, it has never been remembered in any detail in the written histories of Australian rules.

Other sporting calamities have killed more people. In France (1955) a car crashed into a grandstand during the Le Mans race and killed eighty-two spectators; in Peru (1964) a soccer riot killed more than 300 fans; in Scotland (1971) another football fan crush claimed sixty-six lives; and in England (1989) the Hillsborough stadium disaster killed ninety-six people, mostly Liverpool supporters. Soccer fans have been fatally trampled or crushed or burned in many other nations, including Russia (1982), Belgium (1985), Nepal (1988), Guatemala (1996) and Ghana (2001).

Some tragic teams, professional and otherwise, have been immortalised in movies and books after suffering many deaths in accidents. In the United States, the Marshall University football team lost forty-one players when a plane carrying seventy-five people crashed near Huntington, West Virginia, in 1970. A rugby team in Chile (1972) crashed in the Andes – twenty-nine of forty-five aboard were killed. The survivors were not found for months and ate the dead to stay alive.

The Cuban national fencing team died after terrorists blew up a plane off Bridgetown, Barbados, in 1976. There have been others, from Italian football clubs to high school basketball teams.

The most famous sporting accident involved the Manchester United football team, which crashed on its third take-off attempt from Munich airport in 1958. Twenty-three of the forty-four people on board died, including eight players and three officials. It would take manager Matt Busby a decade to rebuild the team to its previous European championship standard.

The shock and grief from the death of one player or coach haunts members of sporting clubs for years. Losing almost an entire team is nearly beyond comprehension.

Mornington went without football for a while. The Rovers were next scheduled to play Frankston in the season 1892. It didn't happen. Anyway, the Rovers experiment was all but over. The sporting townsfolk knew without discussion that when a team from Mornington came onto a field again it would be the one and only.

Mornington decided it would wait until 1893 to resume playing in the local competition, which was becoming more organised by the year. In the meantime, the game came to rescue those suffering financially.

Joseph Worrell and Henry Short led the fundraising effort in the weeks following the Queen's Birthday weekend tragedy, beginning with a public appeal in the metropolitan newspapers. *The Argus* published their letter to the editor. In part, it read:

> The event has plunged the inmates of no fewer than 20 homes into deep mourning and in a small place like this, where almost every other resident has lost a friend or playmate, it is mournful in the extreme . . . Unfortunately this calamity is one which brings distress unto a number of homes . . . We are in a position to state that four widows are left, three of whom with eight young children, are almost destitute, two being enceinte. In addition to these, there are aged parents mourning the loss of sons, who have been of material assistance to them. It was resolved at the meeting that the assistance of the press be sought, and we shall be grateful if you will kindly consent to receive subscriptions on behalf of this most deserving object.

The *Argus* and other newspapers took subscriptions from everywhere. Almost every football club in the colony and some from interstate held concerts and special matches to raise funds for the bereaved. This was even more impressive given the state of Depression, worsening by the month.

Secretaries of all member clubs of the Victorian Football Association held an urgent meeting at Young and

Jackson – the iconic Flinders Street hotel in Melbourne – and set a date for a benefit match. The game would be a contest between representatives from Northern clubs (Carlton, Fitzroy, Essendon, Melbourne, North Melbourne and Collingwood) versus Southern clubs (South Melbourne, Port Melbourne, Williamstown, Footscray, Richmond, St Kilda and Geelong). The team from 'north of the Yarra' would wear Fitzroy colours and the southerners would be in South Melbourne's red and white: Mornington's colours.

The game for the 'Mornington Disaster Fund' went ahead at the Melbourne Cricket Ground on Wednesday 8 June. Three-and-a-half thousand people came to watch. It was free entry but donations were collected outside the venue. This raised one hundred pounds. Players took it easy on one another and anyone expecting a rugged match was disappointed. 'Though the game was a good exhibition . . . there was an absence of keenness which masks the battle for points,' wrote a scribe. But the generosity of football people to help their fellows was astounding. Such a tradition has continued from that day.

Two weeks later another mid-week fundraiser was held, this time at Victoria Park, home of the new Collingwood team, accepted into the Victorian Football Association only a couple of months before the accident. The game was like no other; it was played in fancy dress. The government gave all workers half a day off work and thousands of people came to Hoddle Street to watch the 'gaily and grotesquely attired players as they marched, rode, or were conveyed to the park'.

A police band led a parade to the ground. Players walked behind the musicians in outrageous costumes, dressed as 'pirate kings, Indian warriors, Spanish bravados, John Bull, Sandy McGregor and Ireland's redoubtable St Patrick . . .' When the footballers reached the park they did not change their clothes; rather, they went straight onto the field in their colourful costumes.

Four thousand people watched, laughed and cheered. A boxing match was held at half-time. The fun was interrupted in the second half by an electrical storm. Organisers wondered whether to call it off. The storm would not relent. The wind and rain was causing flash flooding and damage to homes across the city. But the players would not leave the field and continued chasing the leather with paint streaking their faces and outfits falling apart. Another sixty pounds were raised for the people of Mornington, who could only be inspired by the support of their fellow colonists.

Back at The Point, people began emotionally recovering as well as they could. In summer, the hoteliers and boarding-house owners painted their picket fences, cut their grass and waited for the steamers to bring the day-trippers and holiday crowds looking to escape the city heat.

In April 1893, eleven months after the tragedy, the locals finally wanted to play football again. The Mornington Football Club held its first meeting and a scratch match. Former Rovers combined with surviving Mornington players and some newcomers. Enough young men were left over to field a reserves side, referred to as 'Juniors'. Up to a hundred members paid subscriptions.

The *Mornington Standard* reported, 'This certainly is an indication of the interests centred in the club this year, and should the efforts of the M.F.C. in the field be as successful as the enrolments . . . it will have experienced indeed a happy and prosperous season.'

Senior Constable Thomas Murphy chaired the first meeting. Tom Coxhell was named captain.

The first proper match since the accident was a heavy loss to Hastings in May, a week before the first anniversary of the calamity. Coxhell blamed the defeat on the slippery field and difference in weight of the two teams.

A reading of subsequent team lists can reveal one or two Frankston regulars in the side from The Point – another gesture of goodwill.

Mornington slowly improved and beat the town of Dromana before winning against Hastings in a rematch. The first contest against Frankston was not held until late June. The champions of the peninsula enjoyed travelling to Mornington by Millard's four-horse drag. Sadleir starred. Frankston won but not by many goals.

A week later Mornington came up against Mordialloc. To ease the pain of year-old memories, a neutral ground was found. The game went ahead in Frankston. Mornington's match report suggested the club had a breakthrough two-goal victory in fine weather, 'rendering the game a most pleasant one for all concerned'. The Mordialloc report of the same contest differed in tone. The loser accused the winner of 'rough play'. 'In the third quarter the game was a game of "catch as catch can," wrestling, the main object being to hurt one another, everybody being glad when the final bell rang.'

The on-field violence and complaining suggested football, as life, was getting back to normal on the Mornington Peninsula.

On the first anniversary of the day fifteen young men died, a marble monument was erected in Mornington and a ceremony staged at the corner of the Esplanade and Main Street; it stood overlooking the harbour and foreshore as a timeless salute.

Five hundred people heard Rev. Caldwell talk. Thomas and Sarah Allchin were there; J. D. Grover and his family stood by them; Henry Short was at the shoulder of Tom Coxhell, who was near Tom Hutchins and all the other fishermen, including the Hooper adults and children. Senior Constable Murphy was at the front of the crowd. He listened, as they all did, and a silence fell over the gathering. Tears fell from cold faces.

Reverend James Caldwell, with his wife, Marian, daughters Alice, Jeannie and Sallie, and sons Tom (having returned briefly) and Jack by his side, read the following dignified speech in his aging Irish accent. This time his voice did not waver.

> The occasion on which we are met here this day is of a most solemn nature. It is the first anniversary of the event, awful in character and disastrous in effect. By it, a widespread community was brought to mourn, and not a few families to irreparable and lifelong privation and loss. But we are not here today to revive sad feelings, or enlist the sympathy of those around us towards the chief sufferers; that has already been done in an extensive and generous manner. From all parts of this and neighbouring colonies, expressions of heartfelt sympathy have largely been rendered; neither has that fellow feeling been confined to words and letters,

> it has come in the shape of substantial and liberal donations, out of those generous contributions, some who have not only lost dear relations, but their sole breadwinners, have been helped, and only a small portion of the relief fund has been reserved to erect this memorial column and an abiding record of the names of those who perished by the sad event.

It would have been impossible not to look at the sea over the cliffs while he spoke. The victims' families had been 'well-nigh demented' by the sounds of the waves in the past year, But there had been moments of joy, too. Some locals swore there were exactly fifteen baby boys delivered in the twelve months after the accident. One child born late in 1892 was J. D. Grover's son, Roy, now being held in blankets as Rev. Caldwell continued his stirring address.

> A special notice is due to the various football clubs with whom the lost ones were associated [played against]. Next to these, the committee that took charge of the funds, and allotted them, deserve grateful mention. We would be wanting in due acknowledgement, if we passed over our Shire Council, who voted us this appropriate site, and its aid efficiently rendered under the skilful supervision of Mr H. F. Moors, the shire secretary and engineer. With this short detail of history of the sad event, we are here today to commemorate, and now in the name of all concerned, consecrate and dedicate this monument as an abiding tribute of respect to the worth and memory of the cherished loved ones whose name it bears.

People came forward to lay large wreaths, which have long disappeared. But the monument remains in place today, as strong as it was in 1893. Rev. Caldwell also commissioned a memorial tablet to hang in his church. For his sons, he chose the text, 'They were lovely and pleasant in their lives, in their death they were not divided.'

Fifty-two

Of course, twenty-first century Mornington is much different to its early version. But some things have not changed.

After reading about the football tragedy on an information board beside the old marble column, which some people mistake for a war memorial, a modern-day visitor can set off up Main Street on a Saturday afternoon and watch the local football team. The club's earliest football correspondent, Alice Caldwell, once wrote, 'Cheers and groans rent the air.' They still do.

When you arrive at the ground at midday you'll find the dew is gone. The Under-18 team has finished and the reserves side is in action. Hundreds of people and dozens of cars line the steel fence beyond the white painted boundary line. After a goal is scored they honk their horns or shout encouragement. When the umpire makes a mistake, supporters groan and growl.

These days the Mornington Peninsula league is structured into two tiers: Mornington and Mount Eliza are the staunchest rivals and two of the leading clubs. Frankston's population is so large that it has five senior clubs in several levels of competition; the team it fields in Mornington's division – called Frankston YCW – is, like Jack Sadleir's team, the district's undisputed champion. Mornington, Mount Eliza and Frankston teams travel to matches as far north as the suburb of Edithvale, a few kilometres shy of Mordialloc, which plays in another league against suburbs closer to Melbourne. Other peninsula clubs that competed in the 1890s, including Dromana, Hastings, Rosebud and Sorrento, play against each other. The old Flinders club, among others, does not exist.

At 2 pm the senior Mornington team takes the field. The players are dressed in shorts and sleeveless red, white and blue jerseys. The colours were changed from red and white in 1893 and a Bulldog was later chosen as the emblem. The year 1888 has been printed on the present-day uniforms as a nod to the first official season at The Point. The important year is also in bold numerals on the back of the grandstand.

Not much has altered since colonial days in the way football is viewed and played. Participants place great importance on every little moment – ball-ups, throw-ins, free kicks, non-free kicks, bounces and passing – whereas barrackers yearn mostly for collisions, fast goals and spectacular marks. There is handballing now and the kicking is more precise. But the essence of the sport is unchanged since the baker Coxhell led his team and Hugh Caldwell punted straight after the cowbell.

From the spectators' hill in front of the large social club and nearby netball courts, an onlooker can see and hear the effort on the field. The oval is full of young men, mostly muscular and smooth, tattooed-skinned. Their commitment and courage are admirable.

There is a lovely picnicky buzz about the day as light planes scoot by, headed for the coast to see Port Phillip, where remade couta boats are among the sailboats being skippered by people escaping busy work lives and overcrowded streets.

A century and a quarter after Rev. Caldwell said he didn't want Mornington to be a suburb of Melbourne, it has happened. The urban sprawl came through almost twenty years ago. But the sense of a township remains in its people, harbour, beaches, park, bluffs, boats and cliffs, which are the same as they were when Matthew Flinders came to look out from the clearing above the headland.

A hundred shops and a thousand houses separate the shoreline from the football field. All the best old buildings – the Mechanics' Institute, the post office, the Coffee Palace (now the Grand Hotel), the Caldwell house and the Allchin brick tower mansion – are all still standing.

When the football finishes, the crowd makes its way back onto Main Street. Anyone who wants to see where the Caldwells came to live in 1874, after toddler Willie couldn't shake his cough in Maryborough, should turn right at the corner of Barkly Street – where Hugh worked for J. D. Grover – and head along that road. Go past Tanti Avenue, stop walking before the creek, where the boys used to catch eels, and turn right. Look up.

There is the two-storied manse, painted plain white, hemmed in by houses on all sides. The house is a retirement village now. One of the residents, a kind and smiling lady named Win Coates, lives here. Her mother Edith (nee Hirons) grew up in nineteenth-century Mornington and often talked to her daughter about the nights the townsfolk patrolled the cliffs with kerosene lamps, looking for survivors of the *Process*.

Ninety-year-old Mrs Coates remembers summers spent in Mornington. When her family was together on the pier or beaches, Win's mother would look up and tell the story of the search for the footballers, which saddened her forever. But then the family would walk up past the headland, stopping near the memorial to turn and take in the view, as everyone does, and she could remember her childhood in the 1890s. Even as an old lady, she would hold her hands in the air in a fit of nostalgia and say, 'Oh, Mornington . . .'

She thought it was heaven.

Bibliography

Allchin, Charles, The Pelican Reef Disaster, Mornington and District Historical Society, Victoria, 1967.

Anderson, Ross, *Wrecks on the Reef*, Heritage Council Victoria, Melbourne, 1997.

Annear, Robyn, *Bearbrass: Imagining Early Melbourne*, Random House, 1995.

Billot, C. P., *John Batman and the founding of Melbourne*, Hyland House Publishing, 1979.

Blainey, Geoffrey, *A Game of Our Own*, Information Australia, 1990.

Blainey, Geoffrey, *A Shorter History of Australia*, Updated edition, Random House Australia, 2014.

Brookes, Dame Mabel, *Memoirs*, The Macmillan Company of Australia, 1974.

Caldwell, Alice, *Love's Tribute*, the Specialty Press Pty. Limited, Melbourne, 1909.

Chapman, Heather, and Stillman, Judith, *Melbourne Then and Now*, Cameron House, 2007.

Christiansen, Peter, and Ellender, Isabel, *People of the Merri Merri*, Merri Merri Management Committee, 2001.

Collins, Michael, *Our Boys at the Front: The Mornington Peninsula at War*, Mornington and District Historical Society, 2011.

Coker, Evan, Gaskell, John, and Smith, Christopher, *Beneath Our Bay*, Gaskell, Smith and Coker, 2009.

Cotter, Richard, *Boon Wurrung*, second edition, Lavender Hill Multimedia, Red Hill South, Victoria, 2006.

Coventry, James, *Time and Space*, ABC Books, 2015.

Curr, Edward, *Recollections of Squatting in Victoria*, Second edition, reset, Melbourne University Press, 1965.

Davison, Graeme, *The Rise and Fall of Marvellous Melbourne*, Melbourne University Press, 1978.

Dean, Claudia, *William Lindsay*, Claudia Dean, Tasmania (no year listed).

De Araugo, Tess, and Pepper, Phillip, *The Kurnai of Gippsland: Volume One*, Highland House, 1985.

de Moore, Greg, *Tom Wills: His Spectacular Rise and Tragic Fall*, Allen and Unwin, 2008.

Dooley, Sean, *The Big Twitch*, Allen and Unwin, 2005.

Dunstan, Keith, *The Paddock That Grew: The story of the Melbourne Cricket Club*, Cassell Australia, 1974.

Evans, Wilson, *Through the Rip*, Rigby Limited, 1978.

Fitchett, T. K., *Down the Bay*, Rigby Limited, Melbourne, 1973.

Ford, Andrea, *Mornington Pier*, Mornington and District Historical Society, 2007.

Frankston City Council, 'The Families of Ballam Park Homestead', 2007.

Gaynor, Andrew, *The Families of Ballam Park Homestead*, Frankston City Council, Victoria, 2007.

Grishin, Sasha, *S. T. Gill and His Audiences*, National Library of Australia, 2015.

Hansen, Brian, *The Magpies*, Brian Hansen, 1992.

Heads, Ian, and Lester, Gary, *And The Crowd Went Wild*, Playright Publishing, New South Wales, 2010.

Henderson, W. F., and Unstead, R. J., *Pioneer Home Life in Australia*, A. & C. Black Ltd, London, 1971.

Herniman, J. R., *Alfred Dunn*. Other Degree thesis, Faculty of Architecture, Building and Planning, University of Melbourne, 1968.

Hill, David, *Gold*, Random House Australia, 2010.

Howell, Reet, and Howell, Maxwell, *A History of Australian Sport*, Shakespeare Head Press, 1987.

Hume, Fergus, *The Mystery of the Hansom Cab*, Axiom Publishing, 2001.

Innes, Michael and Brunham, Steve, *First Home: the Couta Boat and Victoria's Couta Coast*, Artbytes Communication Pty Ltd, 2005.

Jones, Michael, *Frankston, Resort to City*, Allen and Unwin, 1989.

Lawson, Henry, *A Campfire Yarn: Henry Lawson Complete Works 1885–1900*, Lansdowne, Sydney, 1984.

Leong, Freddie, *Underwater Wonders of the Mornington Pensinula, Victoria, Australia*, Freddie Leong, Victoria, 2010.

McCulloch, Peter, 'Centenarian lost great uncles in football tragedy', *Mornington News*, 2012.

McCulloch, Peter, 'Mornington's Darkest Hour', Peninsula Essence, Victoria, 2015.

Moorhead, Leslie, *Between the Bays*, Loch Haven Books, 1989.

Moorhead, Leslie, *History of Mornington*, Port Phillip Press Pty Ltd, Victoria, 1971.

Mundle, Rob, *Fatal Storm*, HarperCollins, 1999.

Mushins, Eric, *Red and Black: 125 Years of Peninsula Football*, Eric Mushins, Victoria, 2014.

Niall, Brenda, *Georgiana*, Melbourne University Press, Victoria, 1994.

O'Sullivan, J. S., *A Most Unique Ruffian*, F. W. Cheshire, 1968.

Pembroke, Michael, *Arthur Phillip: Sailor, Mercenary, Governor, Spy*, Hardie Grant Books, 2013.

Peters, Mark, *A Voyage to England 1887*, Litera Pty Ltd, 2016.

Prentis, Malcolm, and Ward, Rowland, *Presbyterian Ministers in Australia 1822–1901: Biographical Register*, New Melbourne Press, Melbourne, 2008.

Presland, Gary, *Aboriginal Melbourne*, McPhee Gribble, 1985.

Presland, Gary, *The Land of the Kulin*, McPhee Gribble, 1985.

Rogers, Hunter, *The Early History of Mornington Peninsula, including Frankston and Western Port*, Hunter Rogers, 1957.

Rowe, Susan, and Coleman, Joy, *Hastings Memories: 'Football Memories'*, Hastings-Western Port Historical Society, 2007.

Shillinglaw, John J., Historical Records of Port Phillip, *The First Annals of the Colony of Victoria*, Pioneer Series Edition, William Heinemann Australia, 1972.

Sierp, Allan, *Colonial Life in Victoria*, Rigby Limited, 1972.
Stremski, Brian, *Kill for Collingwood*, Allen and Unwin, 1986.
Taylor, Neil, *The Football Team Disaster* (from Mr Taylor's speech at the tenth Leslie M. Moorhead Memorial Lecture), Mornington and District Historical Society, 1992.
Weaver, *The Criminal of the Century*, Arcadia Australian Scholarly, Melbourne, 2006.

Acknowledgements

I first learned about the Mornington football team tragedy while working as a cadet reporter for the *Mornington Leader* in 1998. The newsroom was a hundred metres from the stone memorial. One autumn day, I wandered from the office to the cliffs and read from the obelisk names of the dead: brothers, fathers, sons, uncles and nephews. As a twenty-two-year-old, who had grown up playing football in the area, I felt like I could see the events of 21 May 1892 – the sailing, tackling, kicking, toasting, singing and drowning – through the eyes of the Caldwells, Charlie Allchin and their mates.

Thereafter, I kept coming back to the story, one way or another. I could not stop wondering why the players never made it back to shore. More than once I swam fully clothed in the bay at the start of winter to test the water's shock; I spent time in libraries looking at newspaper reels; and I spoke to descendants and read their old family letters and diaries. By the age of forty – as the father of three adventurous sons – I could imagine the calamity with a parent's perspective. Also, I was increasingly fascinated by the footballers' lives as much as their deaths. Eventually, I decided to write a book.

Generous people helped me during my research. First thank you goes to local historian Neil Taylor, who wrote a summary of the tragedy for a 100-year anniversary commemoration in 1992. Years ago, Neil allowed me to copy pages from Alice Caldwell's *Love's Tribute*.

Alice wrote her 212-page book in the saddest spring of 1892 but did not have it published until 1909, two years after her father died. This allowed her to add a passage describing Mornington's celebrations on the weekend of Queen Elizabeth's Diamond Jubilee in 1897. Five years after her three brothers died, Alice was in Mornington Park staring at the Chinese lanterns, where she was overcome by the memory of seeing such lights in Melbourne a decade earlier.

> I had only one consolation, and that was I might keep the memory of our dear boys green by placing a cross of fresh flowers on the public monument. In my heart, I thanked God for the long and illustrious reign of our beloved Queen, but blood is thicker than water, or any sentiment, and my thoughts were mostly with my beloved brothers, who had shared my pleasure that day ten years ago.

Alice never married or had children. She died in 1950. The 'little ones' – Jack, Jeannie and Sallie – grew to become impressive young adults, though bad luck continued to cruel the family. Jeannie and Sallie ran a school in Mornington before Jeannie went on an overseas trip and was lost overboard from a ship in the United Kingdom. Her letters home never hinted at unhappiness and her descendants do not believe she ended her own life. Sallie lived to be ninety-one and died in 1973.

Jack Caldwell grew up, moved to Western Australia and finally settled in Gippsland. His brother Tom left Tasmania to join him. The brothers married sisters and farmed the land. Tom lived until 1960, dying two days before his ninety-first birthday. Jack died in 1939 at age fifty-eight from an accidental, self-inflicted gunshot while climbing over a fence. When his longest-surviving child, Jim Caldwell, died in 2012 – aged 101 – the headline in the *Mornington News* obituary read: 'Centenarian lost great uncles in football tragedy.'

I would like to thank Caldwell descendant Janette Allen for her wonderful family photographs and information. Other relatives of nineteenth-century Mornington residents, like Kay and Barry Hooper, Athel and Barry Coxhell, Nigel Peck, John Steele (Rev. White), Neville and Dalton Hutchins, Prue Swann and Lesley and Janet Millar (the Grover family), Claudia Dean (Lindsay family) and Win Coates, have been similarly helpful and encouraging.

Janet Groves, keeper of the Allchin family story, deserves particular praise. She has been incredibly patient and understanding. Her photos and letters are historical treasures and she shared them all. Her assistance gave the memories colour and movement. Janet is a leading member of the Mornington and District Historical Society. Without Janet, as well as lead researchers Diane White and Val Wilson, this book would never have been possible. Historical groups are invaluable to all generations, past and future, and the Mornington executive has to rank among Australia's best.

My research has spanned the decade in which old newspapers have been digitised. Thanks to all the State Library of Victoria staff, who helped me find old reels. And I will be forever grateful to the tireless workers at Trove for transferring all the old *South Bourke and Mornington Journal* and *Mornington Standard* online. The Victorian Public Records Office was a pleasure to visit on many occasions.

The boating community at Mornington was friendly and accommodating in teaching me the thrill of sailing. Twice Peter Sydes took me for a ride in his handsome couta boat with assistance from yachties Trevor Neate, Peter Wood, John Ross, John Vluegel and Graeme Pimlott. Peter even arranged a pod of dolphins to play in our wake – much appreciated!

Yet again, I am indebted to genealogist Sue McBeth, one of the most generous and efficient professionals I have ever met.

Thanks to agent Clare Forster for her constant advice, publisher Nikki Christer, ace editor Patrick Mangan, whose expert guidance was invaluable in telling the story right, and others at Penguin Random House, including Jess Malpass and Judy Jamieson-Green.

Fellow journalists, including Virginia Trioli, Michael Rowland, Tony Jones, Paul Amy, Barrie Cassidy, Vanessa O'Hanlon, Del Irani, Erin Vincent and Tim Lee, were constant sources of support. Virginia: your words, as usual, meant a lot to me.

I wrote this book in many places. I'd like to thank my away-from-home hosts: Mum and Dad, Geoff and Carmel, Nana Cath, Javier and Lana.

A general hats off goes to chief motivator John Holmes, cameraman/editor Craig Johnston, art director Mick Bakos, local scribes Peter McCulloch and Mike Hast, sailing consultant Patrick Bollen, documentary *Ghosts of Australian Football* interviewees Dr Rob Hess and Dr Matthew Klugman, Tim Phillips, and Doug Beazley, Scotch College archivist Paul Mishura, still photographers Joan Kennedy and Jo Quinn, former Mornington FC president Norm Robinson, current MFC president Rob Smith and secretary Alison Dillon, MFC coach Chris Holcolmbe, Mordialloc historians Dr Graham Whitehead and Leo Gamble, and cold water immersion expert Glenn Thompson, among others.

Finally, to my beautiful wife, Kim, and Jack, Gus and Leo: thanks for giving me time, inspiration and hugs.

Paul Kennedy is a national television presenter for ABC News Breakfast. He has worked for three television networks and has written three books, including co-authoring *Hell on the Way to Heaven* (with Chrissie Foster), one of the triggers for Australia's Royal Commission into Institutional Responses to Child Sexual Abuse.

He lives on the eastern shore of Port Phillip with his wife, Kim, and their three sons, Jack, Gus and Leo.